NORDIC KNITS

NORDIC KNITS

25 Stylish, Small Projects

MARTIN STOREY

PHOTOGRAPHS BY
JOHN HESELTINE

St. Martin's Griffin
New York

Nordic Knits
Copyright © 2010 by Berry & Bridges Ltd.
Printed in Singapore. For information, address
St. Martin's Press, 175 Fifth Avenue, New York,
N.Y. 10010.

www.stmartins.com

Library of Congress Cataloging-in-Publication
Data Available Upon Request

ISBN: 978-0-312-64657-8

First U.S. Edition: November 2010

10 9 8 7 6 5 4 3 2 1

CONTENTS

Introduction

My main interest is in fashion knitwear, but my love of knitting has its roots in traditional knitting designs, so creating a collection of 25 or so Nordic-inspired knits with a contemporary twist, in the form of clothing accessories and projects for the home, has been a real treat for me.

What is so great about the Nordic traditions in knitting is firstly their inherent love of good-quality natural yarns, and secondly their abiding interest in textural stitch patterns, along with a great appreciation of wonderful rich but soft colors.

The more northerly countries of Europe—Finland, Norway, Sweden, and the Baltic states, and Great Britain plus the many islands around it, such as the Faroes, the Shetland Isles, the Hebrides and the Orkneys—have reared their own favored breeds of sheep and made use of their wool for clothing for centuries. In their more isolated rural areas, and in the islands, traditional patterns have been handed down more or less unchanged through the generations, in part because of the isolation of some of these communities. Equally, however, these sea-faring nations have influenced each other through bartered goods, so it is hard to trace the ancestry of some of these traditional patterns too exactly.

Home spinning and vegetable-dyed colors produced a wonderful texture and softness to both the fiber and the color palette.

COLORWORK

We are probably most familiar with the colorwork of the Shetland Isles, named after the most southerly island, Fair Isle. Originally Norwegian, the Shetland Isles are now part of Scotland, lying 200 miles north of the mainland and home to the Shetland sheep, a hardy breed with good quality fleece in all shades of gray and brown, from which the island's heritage of knitting has sprung.

The small repeating motifs and shapes were originally worked in undyed fleece, in the round on three needles, which are pointed at both ends. The fabric was therefore seamless and knitted with only plain stitches. The distinctive Fair Isle patterning, as we now know it, involves small repeating motifs

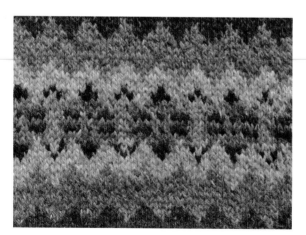

The Fair Isle design of Astrid is typical of traditional diamond-shaped Fair Isle patterns.

The Freya design also uses Fair Isle and similar colorways, but in a more contemporary form.

and shapes in bright colors. Traditionally, only two colors are used on each row, with the yarn not in use being carried across the back of the fabric, known as stranded knitting. The resulting knitted fabric is double thickness, which makes Fair Isle garments very warm and almost weatherproof.

Repeating colors are used across the rows of knitting, so that large loops are not created at the back of the work. Local families traditionally had their own selection of patterns which were passed down from one generation to the next.

In earlier designs, small patterns, two to nine rows deep, were used but gradually larger motifs, like the Norwegian Star, have been incorporated into Fair Isle knitting designs on items such as sweaters, hats, scarves, and gloves.

CABLE PATTERNS

While some communities, such as the Shetland, Norwegian, and Icelandic knitters, have concentrated on colorwork, others have handed down their own patterns using interesting stitch combinations, as found in the fisherman's knitted "ganseys" of the Channel Islands and the wonderful cable patterns of the Aran Islands, near Ireland. These garments were originally knitted by the fishermen themselves, presumably in the long watches on board their fishing boats. Each would have their own pattern variation and rumor has it that each man could be recognized by his particular gansey, or jersey.

Traditionally, an Aran sweater is made from the undyed cream-colored sheep's wool. It is not clear when the Aran islanders started making their now famous cabled sweaters, but by the early 1900s a small group of enterprising island women started creating garments that could be sold as a source of income. These women adapted the traditional gansey sweater by knitting with thicker wool and modifying the construction to increase productivity.

The first commercially available Aran knitting patterns were published in the 1940s by Patons of England and exports of sweaters from the west of Ireland to the United States began in the early 1950s. Each community has developed its own styles and techniques, which gives knitwear designers like myself a wonderful resource to draw from.

The Rowan yarns I have selected for the knits in this book, pay tribute to this heritage of natural yarns. The soft, art-shaded color palette makes it much easier to re-create some of the traditional-style textures and colors.

The Kyrie design employs two different forms of a classic cable stitch.

The twisted stitch of the Pia design is a variation of a cable stitch.

ASTRID

Fair Isle is not only traditional but is one of the most popular forms of colorwork. I love using it as it creates beautifully bright but soft patterns if you choose your colors wisely and don't go for all out contrast. I have used Rowan's Felted Tweed, which is an ideal yarn for these Fair Isles too, as the tweediness resembles the original Shetland yarns and also helps to soften the color. For this set of designs—a scarf, hat, legwarmers, and a vest —I have played with the choice of colors, creating three designs with a dark red ground but choosing a mid-blue ground in the Fair Isle patterning for the legwarmers. There is some advice on page 131 if you are knitting Fair Isle designs for the first time.

20

10

1

12 st rep

KEY

☐ = M

⊡ = A

⬤ = B

◉ = C

☒ = D

◼ = E

⊟ = F

Astrid Scarf

FINISHED SIZE
Approx. 8 x 61½in/20.5 x 156cm

YARN
4 x 1¾oz/197yd balls of Rowan *Felted Tweed* in Rage 150 (M)
1 x 1¾oz/197yd ball each of Rowan *Felted Tweed* in Watery 152 (A), Clay 177 (B), Gilt 160 (C), Avocado 161 (D), Treacle 145 (E), and Melody 142 (F)

NEEDLES
Pair of size 3 (3.25mm) knitting needles
Pair of size 5 (3.75mm) knitting needles

GAUGE
30 sts and 28 rows to 4in/10cm square over patterned St st using size 5 (3.75mm) needles *or size to obtain correct gauge.*

ABBREVIATIONS
See page 133.

NOTE
When working from Chart, K rows read from right to left. P rows read from left to right.
Use the Fair Isle method, strand the yarn not in use across the wrong side of work, weaving it under and over the working yarn every 3 or 4 sts.

SCARF
Using size 5 (3.75mm) needles and M cast on 99 sts.
Row 1 K to end.
Row 2 (inc) P3, [M1, P4] 24 times. *123 sts.*
Cont in patt from Chart.
Row 3 Work first st, then work across 12 st rep patt of row 3 ten times, work last 2 sts.
Row 4 Work first 2 sts, work across 12 st patt rep of row 4 ten times, work last st.
Cont in patt to end of row 20.
Work from Chart row 1 to 20 twice more.
Row 61 (dec) Using M, K3, [K2tog, K3] 24 times. *99 sts.*
Cont in M only.
Starting with a P row cont in St st until scarf measures 51¼in/130cm from cast-on edge, ending with a right side row.
Next row (inc) Using M, P3, [M1, P4] 24 times. *123 sts.*
Turn Chart upside down.
Row 1 Work first 2 sts, work across 12 st patt rep of row 20 ten times, work last st.
Row 2 Work first st, work across 12 st patt rep of row 19 ten times, work last 2 sts.
These 2 rows set the chart.
Cont in patt to end of row 1.
Work from row 20 to 1 twice more.
Next row (dec) Using M, K3, [K2tog, K3] 24 times. *99 sts.*
Next row P to end.
Bind off.

FINISHING
Join row ends together (see page 133).
With seam running down center of back, using size 3 (3.25mm) needles and A, working through both thicknesses, pick up and K48 sts along one short end.
K 6 rows.
Bind off.
Work other end to match.

Astrid Hat

FINISHED SIZE
To fit an average size head, 19¼in/49cm diameter

YARN
1 x 1¾oz/197yd ball each of Rowan *Felted Tweed* in
Rage 150 (M), Watery 152 (A), Clay 177 (B), Gilt
160 (C), Avocado 161 (D), Treacle 145 (E), and
Melody 142 (F)

NEEDLES
Pair of size 3 (3.25mm) knitting needles
Pair of size 5 (3.75mm) knitting needles

GAUGE
30 sts and 28 rows to 4in/10cm square measured
over patterned St st using size 5 (3.75mm) needles
or size to obtain correct gauge.

ABBREVIATIONS
See page 133.

NOTE
When working from Chart, odd numbered rows are
K rows and read from right to left. Even numbered
rows are P rows and read from left to right.
Use the Fair Isle method, strand the yarn not in use
across the wrong side of work weaving it under and
over the working yarn every 3 or 4 sts.

HAT
Using size 3 (3.25mm) needles and M cast on
118 sts.
Row 1 K2, [P2, K2] to end.
Row 2 P2, [K2, P2] to end.
These 2 rows form the rib.
Work a further 3 rows
Row 6 (inc) Rib 2, [M1, rib 4] 29 times. *147 sts.*

Change to size 5 (3.75mm) needles.
Cont in patt from Chart.
Row 1 Work first st, work across 12 st patt rep of
row 1 twelve times, work last 2 sts.
Row 2 Work first 2 sts, work across 12 st patt rep of
row 2 twelve times, work last st.
These 2 rows set the chart.
Cont in patt to end of row 20.
Work from row 1 to 16 again.
Cont in M only.
Next row (dec) K2, [K2tog, K3] 29 times. *118 sts.*
Next row P to end.
Shape crown
Row 1 [K7, K2tog] to last st, K1. *105 sts.*
St st 3 rows.
Row 5 [K6, K2tog] to last st, K1. *92 sts.*
St st 3 rows.
Row 9 [K5, K2tog] to last st, K1. *79 sts.*
St st 3 rows.
Row 13 [K4, K2tog] to last st, K1. *66 sts.*
St st 3 rows.
Row 17 [K3, K2tog] to last st, K1. *53 sts.*
St st 1 row.
Row 19 [K2, K2tog] to last st, K1. *40 sts.*
St st 1 row.
Row 21 [K1, K2tog] to last st, K1. *27 sts.*
Row 22 P1, [P2tog] to end. *14 sts.*
Break off yarn, thread through rem sts, draw up,
and secure.

FINISHING
Join back seam (see page 133).

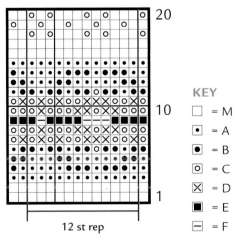

20

10

1

12 st rep

KEY

☐ = M

⊡ = A

⚫ = B

⊙ = C

☒ = D

■ = E

⊟ = F

FAIR ISLE TIP

Practice a small swatch of Fair Isle before you
knit your hat. If your Fair Isle is coming out too
tight, you can increase your needle size just for
the portion of the pattern where you are knitting
in more than one color and then revert to the
correct size for the remainder of the hat. If your
Fair Isle work is too tight, you may notice that the
non-Fair Isle parts "bag" out slightly.

Astrid Legwarmers

FINISHED SIZE

To fit an average woman's (man's) leg
Approx. length 20¾in/53cm

YARN

1 x 1¾oz/197yd ball of Rowan *Felted Tweed* in Rage
150 (M)
2 x 1¾oz/197yd balls of Rowan *Felted Tweed* in
Watery 152 (A)
1 x 1¾oz/197yd ball of Rowan *Felted Tweed* each in
Clay 177 (B), Gilt 160 (C), Avocado 161 (D), Treacle
145 (E), and Melody 142 (F)

KEY
□ = M
· = A
● = B
◉ = C
⊠ = D
■ = E
⊟ = F

12 st rep

NEEDLES

Pair of size 3 (3.25mm) knitting needles
Pair of size 5 (3.75mm) knitting needles

GAUGE

30 sts and 28 rows to 4in/10cm square measured
over patterned St st using size 5 (3.75mm) needles *or
size to obtain correct gauge.*

ABBREVIATIONS

See page 133.

NOTE

When working from Chart, odd numbered rows are
K rows and read from right to left. Even numbered
rows are P rows and read from left to right.
Use the Fair Isle method, strand the yarn not in use
across the wrong side of work weaving it under and
over the working yarn every 3 or 4 sts.

LEGWARMERS (make 2)

Using size 3 (3.25mm) needles and A cast on 90 sts.
Row 1 K2, [P2, K2] to end.
Row 2 P2, [K2, P2] to end.

These 2 rows form the rib.
Work a further 27 rows.
Row 30 (inc) Rib 6, [M1, rib 4] 21 times. *111 sts.*
Change to size 5 (3.75mm) needles and St st.
Cont in patt from Chart.
Row 1 Work first st, work across 12 st patt rep of
row 1 nine times, work last 2 sts.
Row 2 Work first 2 sts, work across 12 st patt rep of
row 2 nine times, work last st.
These 2 rows set the chart.
Cont in patt to end of row 20.
Work from row 1 to 20 four times more.
Row 101 Using M, K to end.
Row 102 Using A, P to end, dec one st at center of
row. *110 sts.*
Row 1 K2, [P2, K2] to end.
Row 2 P2, [K2, P2] to end.
These 2 rows form the rib.
Work a further 28 rows.
Bind off in rib.

FINISHING

Join back seam (see page 133).

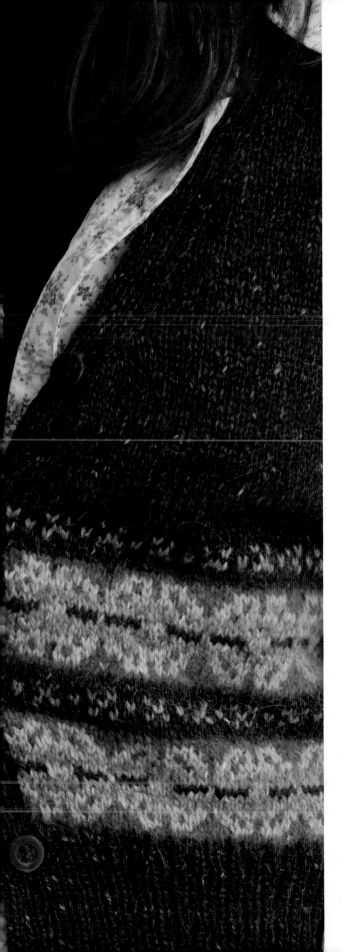

Astrid Vest

TO FIT BUST

32–34	36–38	40–42	in
82–87	92–97	102–10	cm

FINISHED SIZE

Around bust

35½	39½	43½	in
90	100	110	cm

Length to shoulder

19¼	20	20¾	in
49	51	53	cm

YARN

3 (4: 4) x 1¾oz/197yd balls of Rowan *Felted Tweed* in Rage 150 (M)

1 x 1¾oz/197yd ball each of Rowan *Felted Tweed* in Watery 152 (A), Clay 177 (B), Gilt 160 (C), Avocado 161 (D), Treacle 145 (E), and Melody 142 (F)

NEEDLES

Pair of size 3 (3.25mm) knitting needles
Pair of size 5 (3.75mm) knitting needles

EXTRAS

Five buttons, ⅝in/1.5cm diameter

GAUGE

30 sts and 28 rows to 4in/10cm square over patterned St st using size 5 (3.75mm) needles *or size to obtain correct gauge.*
23 sts and 32 rows to 4in/10cm square over St st using size 5 (3.75mm) needles *or size to obtain correct gauge.*

ABBREVIATIONS

See page 133.

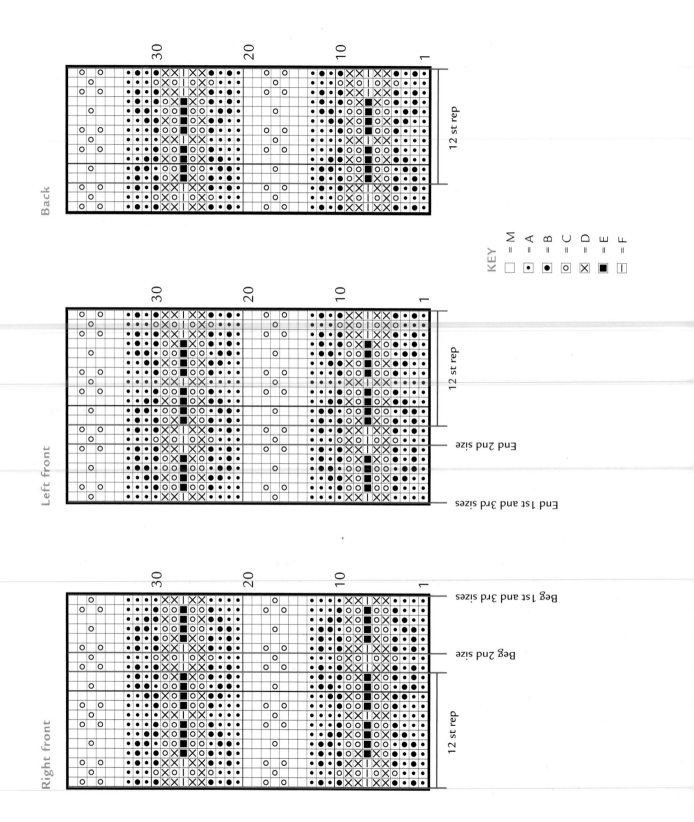

Back

Left front

Right front

KEY

☐ = M
• = A
● = B
○ = C
✕ = D
■ = E
❙ = F

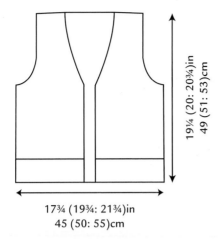

17¾ (19¾: 21¾)in
45 (50: 55)cm

19¼ (20: 20¾)in
49 (51: 53)cm

NOTE

When working from Chart, odd numbered rows are K rows and read from right to left. Even numbered rows are P rows and read from left to right.

Use the Fair Isle method, strand the yarn not in use across the wrong side of work weaving it under and over the working yarn every 3 or 4 sts.

BACK

With size 3 (3.25mm) needles and M, cast on 103 (115: 127) sts.

Row 1 K1, [P1, K1] to end.

Row 2 P1, [K1, P1] to end.

These 2 rows form the rib pattern.

Rep the last 2 rows 13 times more and row 1 again.

Inc row Rib 5 (11: 17), M1, [rib 3, M1] 31 times, rib 5 (11: 17). *135 (147: 159) sts.*

Change to size 5 (3.75mm) needles.

Cont in patt from Chart.

Row 1 Work across 12 st patt rep of row 1 11 (12: 13) times, work last 3 sts.

Row 2 Work first 3 sts, work across 12 st patt rep of row 2 11 (12: 13) times.

These 2 rows set the chart.

Cont to work in patt from Chart to end of row 39.

Cont in M only.

Dec row P4 (10: 16), P2tog, [P2, P2tog] 31 times, P5 (11: 17). *103 (115: 127) sts.*

Cont in St st until back measures 12¼ (12½: 13)in/ 31 (32: 33)cm from cast-on edge, ending with a P row.

Shape armholes

Bind off 9 (10: 11) sts at beg of next 2 rows. *85 (95: 105) sts.*

Next row K1, skp, K to last 3 sts, K2tog, K1.

Next row P1, P2tog, P to last 3 sts, P2tog tbl, P1.

Rep the last 2 rows once more. *77 (87: 97) sts.*

Next row K1, skp, K to last 3 sts, K2tog, K1.

Next row P to end.

Rep the last 2 rows 3 (5: 7) more times. *69 (75: 81) sts.*

Next row K1, skp, K to last 3 sts, K2tog, K1.

Work 3 rows.

Next row K1, skp, K to last 3 sts, K2tog, K1. *65 (71: 77) sts.*

Work even until back measures 19¼ (20: 20¾)in/49 (51: 53)cm from cast-on edge, ending with a P row.

Shape shoulders and back neck

Bind off 5 (6: 7) sts at beg of next 2 rows.

Next row Bind off 5 (6: 7) sts, K until there are 10 sts on the needle, turn and work on these sts for first side of neck.

Next row Bind off 4 sts, patt to end.

Bind off rem 6 sts.

With RS facing, return to rem sts, rejoin yarn, bind off center 25 (27: 29) sts, K to end.

Next row Bind off 5 (6: 7) sts, P to end.

Next row Bind off 4 sts, K to end.

Bind off rem 6 sts.

LEFT FRONT

With size 3 (3.25mm) needles and M, cast on 53 (59: 65) sts.

Row 1 P1, [K1, P1] to end.

Row 2 K1, [P1, K1] to end.

Rep the last 2 rows 13 times more and row 1 again.

Inc row Rib 5 (8: 11), M1, [rib 3, M1] 14 times, rib

6 (9: 12). *68 (74: 80) sts.*

Change to size 5 (3.75mm) needles.

Cont in patt from Chart.

Row 1 Work across 12 st patt rep of row 1, 5 (6: 6) times, work next 8 (2: 8) sts.

This row sets the chart.

Cont to work in patt from Chart to end of row 39.

Cont in M only.

Dec row P3 (6: 9), P2tog, [P2, P2tog] 15 times, P3 (6: 9). *52 (58: 64) sts.*

Cont in St st until front 8 rows less have been worked than back to armhole shaping, ending with a P row.

Shape front neck

Next row K to last 3 sts, K2tog, K1.

Next row P toend.

Rep the last 2 rows 3 times more.

Shape armhole

Next row Bind off 9 (10: 11) sts, K to last 3 sts, K2tog, K1. *38 (43: 48) sts.*

Next row P to end.

Next row K1, skp, K to end.

Next row P to last 3 sts, P2tog tbl, P1.

Next row K1, skp, K to last 3 sts, K2tog, K1.

Next row P to last 3 sts, P2tog tbl, P1. *33 (38: 43) sts.*

Next row K1, skp, K to end.

Next row P to end.

Next row K1, skp, K to last 3 sts, K2tog, K1.

Next row P to end.

Rep the last 4 rows 1 (2: 3) times more. *27 (29: 31) sts.*

Next row K1, skp, K to end.

Next row P to end.

Next row K to last 3 sts, K2tog, K1.

Next row P to end.

Next row K1, skp, K to end. *24 (26: 28) sts.*

Keeping armhole edge straight cont to dec at neck edge on every 4th row until 16 (18: 20) sts rem.

Work even until front measures the same as back to armhole shaping, ending at armhole edge.

Shape shoulder

Next row Bind off 5 (6: 7) sts at beg of next and foll right side row.

Work 1 row.

Bind off rem 6 sts.

RIGHT FRONT

With size 3 (3.25mm) needles and M, cast on 53 (59: 65) sts.

Row 1 P1, [K1, P1] to end.

Row 2 K1, [P1, K1] to end.

Rep the last 2 rows 13 times more and row 1 again.

Inc row Rib 5 (8: 11), M1, [rib 3, M1] 14 times, rib 6 (9: 12). *68 (74: 80) sts.*

Change to size 5 (3.75mm) needles.

Cont in patt from Chart.

Row 1 Work 8 (2: 8) sts before patt rep then work across 12 st patt rep of row 1, 5 (6: 6) times.

Cont to work in patt from Chart to end of row 39.

Cont in M only.

Dec row P3 (6: 9), P2tog, [P2, P2tog] 15 times, P3 (6: 9). *52 (58: 64) sts.*

Cont in St st until front 8 rows less have been worked than back to armhole shaping, ending with a P row.

Shape front neck

Next row K1, skp, K to end.

Next row P to end.

Rep the last 2 rows 3 times more.

Next row K1, skp, K to end.

Shape armhole

Next row Bind off 9 [10: 11] sts, P to end. *38 (43: 48) sts.*

Next row K to last 3 sts, K2tog, K1.

Next row P1, P2tog, P to end.

Next row K1, skp, K to last 3 sts, K2tog, K1.

Next row P1, P2tog, P to end. *33 (38: 43) sts.*

Next row K to last 3 sts, K2tog, K1.

Next row P to end.

Next row K1, skp, K to last 3 sts, K2tog, K1.

Next row P to end.

Rep the last 4 rows 1 (2: 3) more times.
27 (29: 31) sts.
Next row K to last 3 sts, K2tog, K1.
Next row P to end.
Next row K1, skp, K to end.
Next row P to end.
Next row K to last 3 sts, K2tog, K1. *24 (26: 28) sts.*
Keeping armhole edge straight cont to dec at neck edge on every 4th row until 16 (18: 20) sts rem.
Work even until front measures the same as back to armhole shaping, ending at armhole edge.

Shape shoulder
Next row Bind off 5 (6: 7) sts at beg of next and foll wrong side row.
Work 1 row.
Bind off rem 6 sts.

BUTTONBAND
With size 3 (3.25mm) needles and M, cast on 9 sts.
Row 1 K2, [P1, K1] twice, P1, K2.
Row 2 K1, [P1, K1] to end.
Rep the last 2 rows until band, when slightly stretched, fits up left front and halfway round back neck, ending with row 1.
Bind off in rib.
Sew band in place.
Mark position for 5 buttons, the first ¾in/2cm from cast on edge, the 5th ¾in/2cm below neck shaping, and the rem 3 spaced evenly between.

BUTTONHOLE BAND
With size 3 (3.25mm) needles and M, cast on 9 sts.
Row 1 K2, [P1, K1] twice, P1, K2.
Row 2 K1, [P1, K1] to end.
Rep the last 2 rows twice more.
Buttonhole row Rib 4, P2tog, yo, rib 3.
Cont in rib, working buttonholes to match markers, then work even until band, when slightly stretched, fits up right front and halfway round back neck,

ending with row 1.
Bind off in rib.
Sew band in place.

ARMBANDS
Join shoulder seams (see page 133).
With RS facing, using size 3 (3.25mm) needles and M, pick up and K123 (129: 135) sts evenly round armhole edge.
Work 7 rows rib as given for Back.
Bind off in rib.

FINISHING
Join side and armband seams (see page 133).
Join bound-off edges of edging.
Sew on buttons.

CHANGING COLORS

Fair Isle patterns change their appearance a lot if you make even quite small changes of color—say a pale blue for a brighter mid-blue. If you cannot get the precise shade you are looking for (the color may have gone out of stock), you would be better to pick a different color with the same "tonal" value rather than the same one in a brighter shade. You can check the tonal value of any shade by half closing your eyes. At that point, colors with a similar tone will blend. Those that are brighter will stand out much more.

ELLI

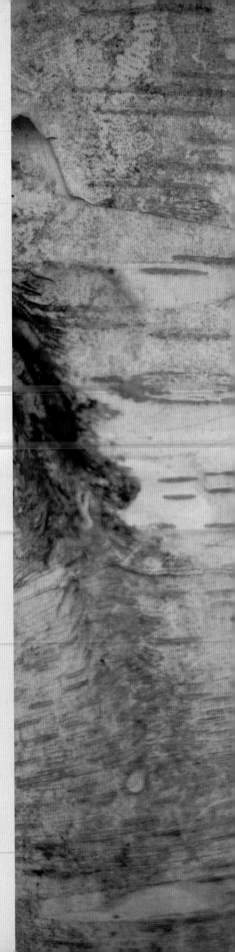

Cables are another great Nordic tradition, popular on the Aran Islands off Ireland. They are used for their cream-colored fisherman's sweaters. I have taken this as inspiration for this classic set of scarf, hat, mittens, and socks, all knitted in Rowan Wool Cotton in Antique— which is a lovely off-white. Worn by Nathalie for a bird-watching trip, the designs would look equally good with a smart town suit. The yarn lends itself to textured stitches, as it is firm enough to hold the shape while still being nice and soft next to the skin.

Elli Scarf

FINISHED SIZE
9 x 67¾in/23 x 172cm (excluding fringe)

YARN
7 x 1¾oz/197yd balls of Rowan *Wool Cotton* in Antique 900

NEEDLES
Pair of size 5 (3.75mm) knitting needles
Cable needle

GAUGE
28 sts and 30 rows to 4in/10cm square measured over patt (slightly stretched) using size 5 (3.75mm) needles *or size to obtain correct gauge.*

ABBREVIATIONS
See page 133.

SPECIAL ABBREVIATIONS
C4B = cable 4 back, slip next 2 sts on a cable needle and leave at back of work, K2, then K2 from cable needle; **C4F** = cable 4 front, slip next 2 sts on a cable needle and leave at front of work, K2, then K2 from cable needle; **C3R** = cross 3 right, slip next st on a cable needle and leave at back of work, K2, then P1 from cable needle; **C3L** = cross 3 left, slip next 2 sts on a cable needle and leave at front of work, P1, then K2 from cable needle.

SCARF
Using size 5 (3.75mm) needles cast on 53 sts.
Row 1 (RS) K to end.
Row 2 [K4, M1] 12 times, K5. *65 sts.*
Cont in patt.
Row 1 K1, P1, K1, P2, [K2, yo, K2tog, P2, C3L, C3R, C3L, P2] 3 times, K2, yo, K2tog, P2, K1, P1, K1.

Row 2 K1, P1, K3, [P2, yo, P2tog, K2, P2, K2, P4, K3] 3 times, P2, yo, P2tog, K3, P1, K1.

Row 3 K1, P1, K1, P2, [K2, yo, K2tog, P3, C4B, P2, K2, P2] 3 times, K2, yo, K2tog, P2, K1, P1, K1.

Row 4 As row 2.

Row 5 K1, P1, K1, P2, [K2, yo, K2tog, P2, C3R, C3L, C3R, P2] 3 times, K2, yo, K2tog, P2, K1, P1, K1.

Row 6 K1, P1, K3, [P2, yo, P2tog, K3, P4, K2, P2, K2] 3 times, P2, yo, P2tog, K3, P1, K1.

Row 7 K1, P1, K1, P2, [C4F, P2, K2, P2, C4F, P3] 3 times, C4F, P2, K1, P1, K1.

Row 8 As row 6.

Row 9 As row 1.

Row 10 As row 2.

Row 11 As row 3.

Row 12 As row 2.

Row 13 As row 5.

Row 14 As row 6.

Row 15 K1, P1, K1, P2, [K2, yo, K2tog, P2, K2, P2, C4F, P3] 3 times, K2, yo, K2tog, P2, K1, P1, K1.

Row 16 As row 2.

These 16 rows form the patt.

Cont in patt until scarf measures 67¾in/172cm from cast-on edge, ending with row 1.

Next row K4, K2tog, [K3, K2tog] 11 times, K4. *53 sts.*

Next row K to end.

Bind off.

FINISHING

Cut 11¾in/30cm lengths of yarn, knot 4 lengths through every other st along cast-on and bound-off edges.

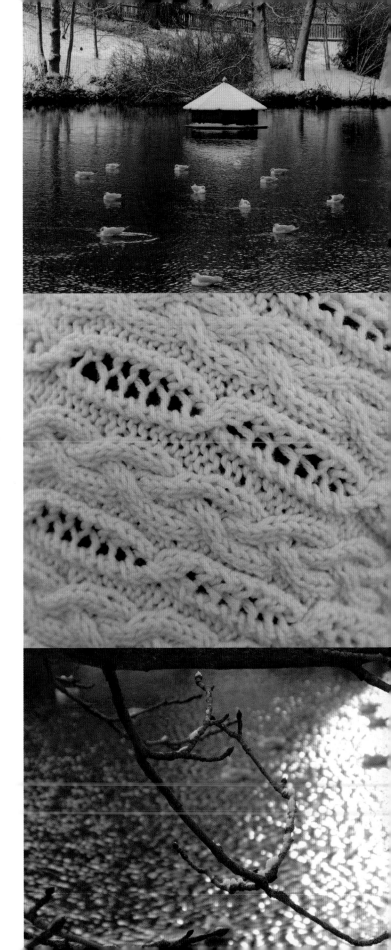

Elli Mittens

FINISHED SIZE

To fit an average small-med (med-large) hand
Approx. length 11 (11¾)in/28 (30)cm

YARN

2 x 1¾oz/197yd balls of Rowan *Wool Cotton* in
Antique 900

NEEDLES

Pair of size 3 (3.25mm) knitting needles
Pair of size 5 (3.75mm) knitting needles
Cable needle

GAUGE

28 sts and 30 rows to 4in/10cm square measured
over patt (slightly stretched) using size 5 (3.75mm)
needles *or size to obtain correct gauge.*

ABBREVIATIONS

See page 133.

SPECIAL ABBREVIATIONS

C4B = cable 4 back, slip next 2 sts on a cable needle
and leave at back of work, K2, then K2 from cable
needle; **C4F** = cable 4 front, slip next 2 sts on a cable
needle and leave at front of work, K2, then K2 from
cable needle; **C3R** = cross 3 right, slip next st on a
cable needle and leave at back of work, K2, then P1
from cable needle; **C3L** = cross 3 left, slip next 2 sts
on a cable needle and leave at front of work, P1, then
K2 from cable needle.

LEFT MITTEN

Using size 3 (3.25mm) needles cast on 60
(68) sts.
Row 1 (RS) [P2, K2] to end.
Rep the last row for 1in/2.5cm, ending with a wrong

side row, dec 0 (1) st in center of last row.
60 (67) sts.
Change to size 5 (3.75mm) needles.
Cont in patt.
Row 1 P3 (4), [K2, yo, K2tog, P3 (4), C3L, C3R,
C3L, P3 (4)] to end.
Row 2 K3 (4), [P2, K2, P4, K4 (5), P2, yo, P2tog, K3
(4)] to end.
Row 3 P3(4), [K2, yo, K2tog, P4 (5), C4B, P2, K2,
P3 (4)] to end.
Row 4 As row 2.
Row 5 P3 (4), [K2, yo, K2tog, P3 (4), C3R, C3L,
C3R, P3 (4)] to end.
Row 6 [K4 (5), P4, K2, P2, K3 (4), P2, yo, P2tog] to
last 3 (4) sts, K3 (4).
Row 7 P3 (4), [C4F, P3 (4), K2, P2, C4F, P4 (5)]
to end.
Row 8 As row 6.
Row 9 As row 1.
Row 10 As row 2.
Row 11 As row 3.
Row 12 As row 2.
Row 13 As row 5.
Row 14 As row 6.
Row 15 P3 (4), [K2, yo, K2tog, P3 (4), K2, P2, C4F,
P4 (5)] to end.
Row 16 As row 2.
Dec row P1 (2), P2tog tbl, [K2, yo, K2tog, P3 (4),
C3L, C3R, C3L, P1 (2), P2tog] to end. *56 (63) sts.*
Patt 5 rows as set.
Dec row P2 (3), [C4F, P1 (2), P2tog, K2, P2, C4F,
P3 (4)] to end. *53 (60) sts.*
Patt 5 rows as set.
Shape for thumb
Row 1 Patt 23 (27), inc in next st, patt to end.
54 (61) sts.
Row 2 Patt 30 (34), place marker on needle, P1,

28

place marker on needle, patt to end.

** **Row 3** Patt to marker, slip marker onto right hand needle, M1, K1, M1, slip marker onto right hand needle, patt to end.

Row 4 Patt to end, slipping markers, working thumb sts in St st.

Row 5 Patt to marker, slip marker onto right hand needle, M1, K to next marker, M1, slip marker onto right hand needle, patt to end.

Row 6 Patt to end, slipping markers.

Row 7 Patt to marker, slip marker onto right hand needle, K to next marker, slip marker onto right hand needle, patt to end.

Row 8 Patt to end, slipping markers.

Row 9 Patt to marker, slip marker onto right hand needle, M1, K to next marker, M1, slip marker onto

right hand needle, patt to end.

Row 10 Patt to end, slipping markers.

Rows 11 to 22 Rep rows 5 to 10 twice more. *68 (76) sts.*

2nd size only

Rep rows 5 to 6 once more. *77 sts.*

Both sizes

Thumb shaping

Next row Patt to marker, slip marker onto right hand needle, K to next marker, turn.

Next row P to marker, turn. *15 (17) sts.*

Beg with a K row, cont in St st.

Work 14 (16) rows.

Shape top

Next row K0 (1), [K1, K2tog] 5 times, K0 (1). *10 (12) sts.*

P 1 row.

Next row [K2tog] 5 (6) times. *5 (6) sts.*

Break off yarn thread through rem sts, draw up and fasten off.

Join thumb seam.

With RS facing, rejoin yarn to rem sts, patt to end. *53 (60) sts.*

Cont in patt until mitten measures 9½ (9¾)in/24 (25)cm from cast-on edge, ending with a WS row **.

Shape top

Counting from beg of last (WS) row place a marker between 29th (33rd) and 30th (34th) sts on needle.

Next row K1, skp, patt to within 2 sts of marker, K2tog, slip marker, skp, patt to last 3 sts, K2tog, K1.

Next row P2, patt to within one st of marker, P1, slip marker, P1, patt to last 2 sts, P2.

Rep the last 2 rows 5 (6) times more and the first row again. *25 (28) sts.*

Bind off.

RIGHT MITTEN

Using size 3 (3.25mm) needles cast on 60 (68) sts.

Row 1 (RS) [P2, K2,] to end.

Rep the last row for 1in/2.5cm, ending with a WS row, dec 0 (1) st in center of last row. *60 (67) sts.*

Change to size 5 (3.75mm) needles.

Cont in patt.

Row 1 P3 (4), [C3L, C3R, C3L, P3 (4), K2, yo, K2tog, P3 (4)] to end.

Row 2 K3 (4), [P2, yo, P2tog, K3 (4), P2, K2, P4, K4 (5)] to end.

Row 3 P3 (4), [P1, C4B, P2, K2, P3 (4), K2, yo, K2tog, P3 (4)] to end.

Row 4 As row 2.

Row 5 P3 (4), [C3R, C3L, C3R, P3 (4), K2, yo, K2tog, P3 (4)] to end.

Row 6 [K3 (4), P2, yo, P2tog, K4 (5), P4, K2, P2] to last 3 (4) sts, K3 (4).

Row 7 P3 (4), [K2, P2, C4F, P4(5), C4F, P3 (4)] to end.

Row 8 As row 6.

Row 9 As row 1.

Row 10 As row 2.

Row 11 As row 3.

Row 12 As row 2.

Row 13 As row 5.

Row 14 As row 6.

Row 15 P3 (4), [K2, P2, C4F, P4 (5), K2, yo, K2tog, P3 (4)] to end.

Row 16 As row 2.

Dec row P1 (2), P2tog, [C3L, C3R, C3L, P2tog, P1(2), K2, yo, K2tog, P3 (4)] to end. *56 (63) sts.*

Patt 5 rows as set.

Dec row P2 (3), [K2, P2, C4F, P1(2), P2tog tbl, P1 (2), C4F, P3(4)] to end. *53 (60) sts.*

Patt 5 rows as set.

Shape for thumb

Row 1 Patt 29 (33), inc in next st, patt to end. *54 (61) sts.*

Row 2 Patt 23 (26), place marker on needle, P1, place marker on needle, patt to end.

Work as given for Left Mitten from ** to **.

Shape top

Counting from beg of last (WS) row place a marker between 24th (27th) and 25th (28th) sts on needle.

Next row K1, skp, patt to within 2 sts of marker, K2tog, slip marker, skp, patt to last 3 sts, K2tog, K1.

Next row P2, patt to within one st of marker, P1, slip marker, P1, patt to last 2 sts, P2.

Rep the last 2 rows 5 (6) times more and the first row again. *25 (28) sts.*

Bind off.

FINISHING

Join top and side seam (see page 133).

Elli Hat

FINISHED SIZE

To fit an average size head, 19¼in/49cm diameter

YARN

2 x 1¾oz/197yd balls of Rowan *Wool Cotton* in Antique 900

NEEDLES

Pair of size 5 (3.75mm) knitting needles
Cable needle

GAUGE

28 sts and 30 rows to 4in/10cm square measured over patt (slightly stretched) using size 5 (3.75mm) needles *or size to obtain correct gauge*.

ABBREVIATIONS

See page 133.

SPECIAL ABBREVIATIONS

C4B = cable 4 back, slip next 2 sts on a cable needle and leave at back of work, K2, then K2 from cable needle; **C4F** = cable 4 front, slip next 2 sts on a cable needle and leave at front of work, K2, then K2 from cable needle; **C3R** = cross 3 right, slip next st on a cable needle and leave at back of work, K2, then P1 from cable needle; **C3L** = cross 3 left, slip next 2 sts on a cable needle and leave at front of work, P1, then K2 from cable needle.

HAT

Using size 5 (3.75mm) needles cast on 138 sts.
Row 1 (RS) P2, [K2, P2] to end.
Row 2 K2, [P2, K2] to end.
Rep the last 2 rows for 1¼in/3cm, ending with row 2.
Cont in patt.

Row 1 P2, [K2, yo, K2tog, P2, C3L, C3R, C3L, P2] to end.
Row 2 K2, [P2, K2, P4, K3, P2, yo, P2tog, K2] to end.
Row 3 P2, [K2, yo, K2tog, P3, C4B, P2, K2, P2] to end.
Row 4 As row 2.
Row 5 P2, [K2, yo, K2tog, P2, C3R, C3L, C3R, P2] to end.
Row 6 [K3, P4, K2, P2, K2, P2, yo, P2tog] to last 2 sts, K2.
Row 7 P2, [C4F, P2, K2, P2, C4F, P3] to end.
Row 8 As row 6.
Row 9 As row 1.
Row 10 As row 2.
Row 11 As row 3.
Row 12 As row 2.
Row 13 As row 5.
Row 14 As row 6.
Row 15 P2, [K2, yo, K2tog, P2, K2, P2, C4F, P3] to end.
Row 16 As row 6.
Rows 17 to 32 As rows 1 to 16.

Shape top

Row 1 P2tog, [K2, yo, K2tog, P2tog, C3L, C3R, C3L, P2tog] to end. *121 sts.*
Row 2 K1, [P2, K2, P4, K2, P2, yo, P2tog, K1] to end.
Row 3 P1, [K2, yo, K2tog, P2, C4B, P2, K2, P1] to end.
Row 4 As row 2.
Row 5 P1, [K2, yo, K2tog, P1, C3R, C3L, C3R, P1] to end.
Row 6 [K2, P4, K2, P2, K1, P2, yo, P2tog] to last st, K1.
Row 7 P1, [C4F, P1, K2, P2, C4F, P2tog] to end. *113 sts.*

Row 8 [K1, P4, K2, P2, K1, P2, yo, P2tog] to last st, K1.

Row 9 P1, [K2, yo, K2tog, P1, K1, skp, K2, K2tog, K1, P1] to end. *97 sts.*

Row 10 K1, [p6, K1, P2, yo, P2tog, K1] to end.

Row 11 P1, [K2, yo, K2tog, P1, K1, skp, K1, K2tog, P1] to end. *81 sts.*

Row 12 K1, [P4, K1, P2, yo, P2tog, K1] to end.

Row 13 P1, [K2, yo, K2tog, P1, skp, K2tog, P1] to end. *65 sts.*

Row 14 K1, [P2, K1, P2, yo, P2tog, K1] to end.

Row 15 P1, [K1, K2tog, K1, P1, K2, P1] to end. *57 sts.*

Row 16 K1, [P2, K1, P3, K1] to end.

Row 17 P1, [K2tog, K1, P1, K2, P1] to end. *49 sts.*

Row 18 K1, [P2, K2] to end.

Row 19 P1, [K2tog, P1] to end. *33 sts.*

Row 20 P1, [P2tog] 16 times. *17 sts.*

Leaving a long end, break off yarn, thread through rem sts, and fasten off securely.

FINISHING

Join seam (see page 133).

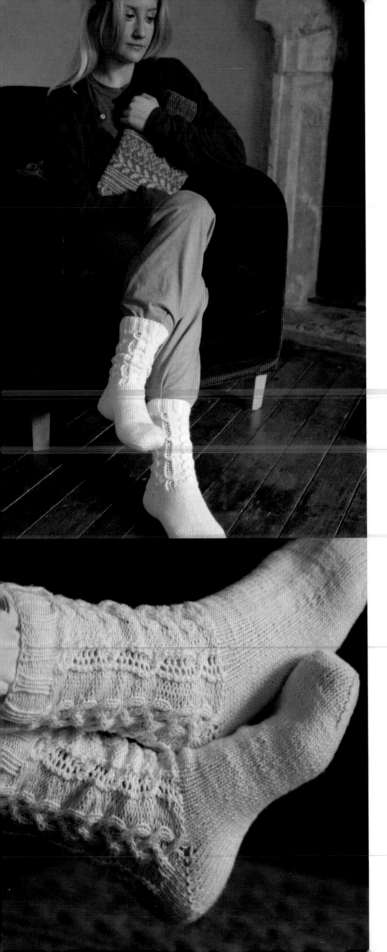

Elli Socks

FINISHED SIZE

To fit shoe size: US 6½–7½ (8½–9½)/UK 4–5 (6–7)
Length from base of heel: 9 (9½)in/23 (24)cm

YARN

3 x 1¾oz/197yd balls of Rowan *Wool Cotton* in
Antique 900

NEEDLES

Set of size 3 (3.25mm) double-pointed knitting
needles
Set of size 5 (3.75mm) double-pointed knitting
needles
Cable needle

GAUGE

28 sts and 30 rows to 4in/10cm square measured
over patt (slightly stretched) using size 5 (3.75mm)
needles *or size to obtain correct gauge.*

ABBREVIATIONS

See page 133.

SPECIAL ABBREVIATIONS

C4B = cable 4 back, slip next 2 sts on a cable
needle and leave at back of work, K2, then K2
from cable needle; **C4F** = cable 4 front, slip next
2 sts on a cable needle and leave at front of work,
K2, then K2 from cable needle; **C3R** = cross 3 right,
slip next st on a cable needle and leave at back of
work, K2, then P1 from cable needle; **C3L** = cross
3 left, slip next 2 sts on a cable needle and leave
at front of work, P1, then K2 from cable needle;
wrap 1 = with yarn to front, slip next st, turn, bring
yarn to front, slip st back onto right hand needle.

SOCKS (make 2)

Using size 3 (3.25mm) needles cast on 56 sts.

Distribute sts on 3 needles

Round 1 (RS) [K2, P2] to end.

Rep the round for 1½in/4cm, inc one st in center of last round. *57 sts.*

Change to size 5 (3.75mm) needles.

Cont in patt.

Round 1 [P3, K2, yo, K2tog, P3, C3L, C3R, C3L] to end.

Round 2 [P3, K2tog, yo, K2, P4, K4, P2, K2] to end.

Round 3 [P3, K2, yo, K2tog, P4, C4B, P2, K2] to end.

Round 4 As round 2.

Round 5 [P3, K2, yo, K2tog, P3, C3R, C3L, C3R] to end.

Round 6 [P3, K2tog, yo, K2, P3, K2, P2, K4, P1] to end.

Round 7 [P3, C4F, P3, K2, P2, C4F, P1] to end.

Round 8 As round 6.

Round 9 As round 1.

Round 10 As round 2.

Round 11 As round 3.

Round 12 As round 2.

Round 13 As round 5.

Round 14 As round 6.

Round 15 [P3, K2, yo, K2tog, P3, K2, P2, C4F, P1] to end.

Round 16 As round 6.

Rounds 17 to 32 As rounds 1 to 16.

Dec round [P1, P2tog, K2, yo, K2tog, P3, C3L, C3R, C3L] to end. *54 sts.*

Patt 15 rounds as set.

Dec round [P2, K2, yo, K2tog, P1, P2tog, C3L, C3R, C3L] to end. *51 sts.*

Patt 15 rounds as set.

Cut yarn.

Shape heel

Slip next 13 sts on first needle, next 13 sts on second needle, next 13 sts on 3rd needle, and last 12 sts on end of first needle.

Rejoin yarn to beg of first needle.

Next row K24, wrap 1.

Next row P23, wrap 1.

Next row K22, wrap 1.

Next row P21, wrap 1.

Cont in this way, working one less st on every row until the foll row has been worked:

Next row P11, wrap 1.

Next row K11, wrap 1.

Next row P12, wrap 1.

Cont in this way, working one more st on every row until the foll row has been worked:

Next row K23, wrap 1.

Next row P24, wrap first st on next needle.

With RS facing, slip next 17 sts on first needle, next 17 sts on second needle and next 17 sts on third needle.

Cont in rounds of St st until sock measures 5½ (6) in/14 (15)cm from last dec row, dec one st at end of last round. *50 sts.*

Shape toe

Next round [K1, skp, K19, K2tog, K1] twice.

Next round K to end.

Next round [K1, skp, K17, K2tog, K1] twice.

Next round K to end.

Next round [K1, skp, K15, K2tog, K1] twice.

Next round K to end.

Cont in rounds dec on every alt round as set until the foll round has been worked.

Next round [K1, skp, K7, K2tog, K1] twice.

Slip first 11 sts onto one needle and rem 11 sts onto a second needle.

Fold sock inside out and bind one st from each needle off together.

INGA

This generous, heavily textured floor cushion is both

comfortable and comforting. It is knitted in Rowan

Felted Twee hion pad with a toning cotton cover

to prevent the white pad showing through the lacy

holes. The cushion cover is fastened at the back with

a simple ribbed buttonband, like the other cushions

in this book.

FINISHED SIZE
Approx. 30in/76cm square

YARN
22 x 1¾oz/197yd balls of Rowan *Felted Tweed Chunky*
in Clay 281

NEEDLES
Pair of size 11 (8mm) knitting needles
Cable needle

EXTRAS
Eight buttons, 1in/2.5cm diameter
30in/76cm cushion pad

GAUGE
11 sts and 14 rows to 4in/10cm square measured
over St st using size 11 (8mm) needles *or size to obtain
correct gauge.*
15 sts and 15 rows to 4in/10cm square measured
over patt using size 11 (8mm) needles *or size to obtain
correct gauge.*

ABBREVIATIONS
See page 133.

SPECIAL ABBREVIATIONS
C6B = cable 6 back, slip next 3 sts on a cable needle
and leave at back of work, K3, then K3 from cable
needle; **C6F** = cable 6 front, slip next 3 sts on a
cable needle and leave at front of work, K3, then K3
from cable needle.

FRONT
Using size 11 (8mm) needles cast on 83 sts.
Row 1 (RS) K to end.
Inc row [K3, M1] 8 times, [K2, M1] 16 times, [K3,
M1] 8 times, K3. *115 sts.*
Cont in patt.
Row 1 P1, K1, [skp, yo, K12] to last st, P1.
Row 2 and every foll alt row K2, [P2tog, yo, P11,

K1] to last st, K1.

Row 3 P1, K1, [skp, yo, C6B, K6] to last st, P1.

Row 5 As row 1.

Row 7 P1, K1, [skp, yo, K3, C6F, K3] to last st, P1.

Row 8 As row 2.

These 8 rows form the patt.

Rep rows 1 to 8 twelve times more, then row 1 again.

Dec row [K2, K2tog] 8 times, [K1, K2tog] 16 times, [K2, K2 tog] 8 times, K3. *83 sts.*

Next row K to end.

Bind off.

BACK

Lower Back

Using size 11 (8mm) needles cast on 83 sts.

Beg with a K row, work 46 rows in St st.

Row 1 K4, [P3, K3] to last 7 sts, P3, K4.

Row 2 P4, [K3, P3] to last 7 sts, K3, p4.

These 2 rows form the rib.

Work a further 14 rows.

Bind off in rib.

Upper Back

Using size 11 (8mm) needles cast on 83 sts.

Row 1 K4, [P3, K3] to last 7 sts, P3, K4.

Row 2 P4, [K3, P3] to last 7 sts, K3, P4.

These 2 rows form the rib.

Work a further 6 rows.

Buttonhole row Rib 6, [work 2 tog, yo, rib 8] 7 times, work 2 tog, yo, rib 5.

Work a further 7 rows.

Beg with a K row, work 46 rows in St st.

Bind off.

FINISHING

Lay front RS up. Position upper back on top of front, RS together. Position lower back on top of front RS together, overlapping rib. Sew back to front. Turn to RS, sew on buttons.

Insert cushion pad.

FOLKIE

This hot-water bottle cover has
a beautiful traditional Fair Isle
pattern, which I have chosen to
do using just two colors—a soft
raspberry and a clay color. There
is nothing nicer than a hot-water
bottle with a pretty, cozy cover on
a cold night! The pattern would be
great for a scarf too, and as the
bottle cover is about 9in/23cm
wide, it would make a good width
for a scarf. You could knit it double
like the Astrid scarf (see page 11),
and just use the Fair Isle pattern at
either end of a plain scarf.

FINISHED SIZE

9 x 9¾in/23 x 25cm

YARN

1 x 1¾oz/197yd ball each of Rowan *Felted Tweed* in Paisley 171 (A) and Clay 177 (B)

NEEDLES

Pair of size 3 (3.25mm) knitting needles
Pair of size 5 (3.75mm) knitting needles

EXTRAS

Three buttons, ⅝in/1.5cm diameter

GAUGE

23 sts and 32 rows to 4in/10cm square measured over St st using size 5 (3.75mm) needles *or size to obtain correct gauge.*

ABBREVIATIONS

See page 133.

NOTE

When working from Chart, odd numbered rows are K rows and read from right to left. Even numbered rows are P rows and read from left to right.

Use the Fair Isle method, strand the yarn not in use across the wrong side of work weaving it under and over the working yarn every 3 or 4 sts.

FRONT

Using size 5 (3.75mm) needles and A cast on 45 sts.
Row 1 Using A, K to end.
Cont in patt from Chart shaping as shown.
Bind off.

BACK

Lower Back

Using size 5 (3.75mm) needles and A cast on 45 sts.
Row 1 Using A, K to end.
Cont in patt from row 2 of Chart to end of row 40,

shaping as shown.
Cont in A only.
Work 2 rows St st.
Change to size 3 (3.25mm) needles.
Row 1 P3, [K3, P3] to end.
Row 2 K3, [P3, K3] to end.
These 2 rows form the rib.
Work a further 6 rows.
Bind off in rib.

Upper Back

Using size 3 (3.25mm) needles and A cast on 63 sts.
Row 1 P3, [K3, P3] to end.
Row 2 K3, [P3, K3] to end.
These 2 rows form the rib.
Work a further 2 rows.
Buttonhole row Rib 6, [P2tog, yo, rib 22] twice, P2tog, yo, rib 7.
Work a further 3 rows.
Change to size 5 (3.75mm) needles.
Beg with a K row, beg at row 51 cont in patt from chart shaping as shown.
Bind off.

COLLAR

Join left "shoulder" seam.
With RS facing using size 3 (3.25mm) needles and A, pick up and K 25 sts from upper back then 25 sts from front. *50 sts.*
Row 1 K4, [P3, K3] to last 4 sts, P4.
This row forms the rib.
Cont in rib until collar measures 3¼in/8cm.
Change to size 5 (3.75mm) needles.
Worker a further 3¼in/8cm.
Bind off in rib.

FINISHING

Lap upper back rib over lower back rib and baste in place. With RS together, sew back to front, reversing final 4in/10cm of collar seam for fold back. Turn to RS, sew on buttons.

KEY   □ = A
      ☒ = B

CHORA

This very simple shrug, knitted in stockinette stitch, is a good choice for a relatively inexperienced knitter. It is also pretty forgiving on shape if your gauge is a bit out, too. The yarn, Rowan's ever popular Kidsilk Haze, is just great for this kind of garment as it is warm, light, and soft. Just what you want for a little cover up to go over a camisole or a light summer dress.

TO FIT BUST

S	M	L	XL	

FINISHED SIZE
Around bust

35	41	46½	52	in
90	104	118	132	cm

Length to shoulder

15	15¾	16½	17¼	in
38	40	42	43.5	cm

Cuff to cuff (excluding edging)

49¼	52	54¾	57½	in
125	132	139	146	cm

YARN

4 (5: 5: 6) x ⅞oz/229yd balls of Rowan *Kidsilk Haze* in Dewberry 600

NEEDLES

Pair of size 2 (2.75mm) knitting needles
Pair of size 3 (3.25mm) knitting needles
Size 3 (3.25mm) circular needle

GAUGE

25 sts and 34 rows to 4in/10cm over St st using size 3 (3.25mm) needles *or size to obtain correct gauge.*

ABBREVIATIONS

See page 133.

FRONTS, SLEEVES, AND BACK
Left front and sleeve

With size 3 (3.25mm) needles cast on 55 (62: 69: 76) sts.
Beg with a K row cont in St st.
Work 6 (8: 10: 12) rows.
Front neck shaping
Row 1 (RS) K to last 2 sts, K2tog.
Work 5 rows.
Rep the last 6 rows three times more.
Shape sleeve

Next row K1, M1, K to last 2 sts, K2tog.
This row sets the armhole shaping.
Cont to dec at neck edge on the 14 foll 6th rows at the same time inc at armhole edge on 2 foll 4th rows then 15 foll alt rows, ending with a RS row.
Now inc at armhole edge on next 12 rows.
Next row P to end.
Underarm shaping

Cast on 10 sts at beg of next row and 20 sts at beg of foll 3 right side rows.
Keeping sleeve edge straight cont to dec at neck edge until all 19 decs have been worked.
136 (143: 150: 157) sts.
Work 6 (10: 14: 18) rows, ending with a K row.
Leave these sts on a spare needle.
Right front and sleeve

With size 3 (3.25mm) needles cast on 55 (62: 69: 76) sts.
Beg with a K row cont in St st.
Work 6 (8: 10: 12) rows.
Front neck shaping

Row 1 (RS) Skp, K to end.
Work 5 rows.
Rep the last 6 rows three times more.
Shape sleeve

Next row Skp, K to last st, M1, K1.
This row sets the armhole shaping.
Cont to dec at neck edge on the 14 foll 6th rows **at the same time** inc at armhole edge on 2 foll 4th rows then 15 foll alt rows, ending with a RS row.
Now inc at armhole edge on next 12 rows.
Next row P to end.
Next row K to end.
Underarm shaping

Cast on 10 sts at beg of next row and 20 sts at each end of foll 3 WS rows.
Keeping sleeve edge straight cont to dec at neck edge until all 19 decs have been worked.
136 (143: 150: 157) sts.
Work 6 (10: 14: 18) rows, ending with a K row.

Back and sleeves

Change to circular needle.

Next row P across 136 (143: 150: 157) sts of right front, cast on 40 (44: 48: 52) sts, P across 136 (143: 150: 157) sts on left front.

Work 40 (44: 48: 52) rows even.

Underarm shaping

Bind off 20 sts at beg of next 6 rows and 10 sts at beg of foll 2 rows.

Dec one st at each end of next 13 rows then 15 foll RS rows and 2 foll 4th rows.

Work 23 (25: 27: 29) rows even, ending with a P row.

Bind off.

NECK TRIM

With size 2 (2.75mm) needles cast on 13 sts.

Row 1 K2, [P1, K1] to last 3 sts, P1, K2.

Row 2 K1, [P1, K1] to end.

These 2 rows form the rib.

Cont in rib until trim fits up left front, round back neck, and down right front.

Bind off.

HEM TRIM AND TIES

With size 2 (2.75mm) needles cast on 13 sts.

Row 1 K2, [P1, K1] to last 3 sts, P1, K2.

Row 2 K1, [P1, K1] to end.

These 2 rows form the rib.

Cont in rib until tie measures 23½in/60cm long, place a marker at beg of last row. Cont in rib until trim fits along cast-on edge of left front, bound-off edge of back, and cast-on edge of right front, place a marker at beg of last row. Work a further 23½in/60cm in rib for second tie.

Bind off.

SLEEVE TRIMS

With size 2 (2.75mm) needles cast on 13 sts.

Row 1 K2, [P1, K1] to last 3 sts, P1, K2.

Row 2 K1, [P1, K1] to end.

These 2 rows form the rib.

Cont in rib until trim fits along row ends of sleeves.

Bind off.

FINISHING

Sew neck trim and sleeve trims in place.

Join side and underarm seams (see page 133).

Sew hem trim between markers. Knot ties in a bow.

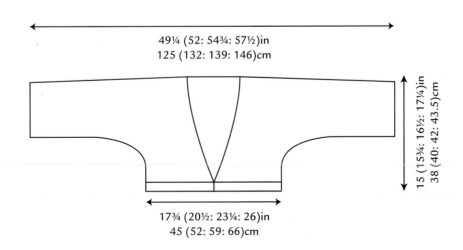

49¼ (52: 54¾: 57½)in
125 (132: 139: 146)cm

15 (15¾: 16½: 17¼)in
38 (40: 42: 43.5)cm

17¾ (20½: 23¼: 26)in
45 (52: 59: 66)cm

FREYA

This bag is a contemporary take on Fair Isle and looks pretty cool, I think, thanks partly to the contrasts of circles and stripes in the design, and also the choice of the green, pink, and magenta. Not your traditional color choices. As the bag is fairly small, it makes a good choice of project for your first attempt at Fair Isle work, but you do need to take care when working with two colors in one row that you do not pull the yarns too tight when you strand them across the back. Morwenna, the model, is wearing the Thora shrug (see page 46).

FINISHED SIZE
Approx. 8¼ x 9¾in/21 x 25cm

YARN
1 x 1¾oz/197yd ball each of Rowan *Felted Tweed* in Treacle 145 (A), Avocado 161(C), Rage 150 (D), and Melody 142 (E)
Small amount of Rowan *Felted Tweed* in Carbon 159 (B)

NEEDLES
Pair of size 5 (3.75mm) knitting needles

EXTRAS
Pair of plastic ring handles, approx. 6¼ x 4¾in/ 5.5 x 12cm
Lining fabric, 19¾ x 11¾in/50 x 30cm

GAUGE
30 sts and 28 rows to 4in/10cm square over patterned St st using size 5 (3.75mm) needles *or size to obtain correct gauge.*

ABBREVIATIONS
See page 133.

NOTE
When working from Chart, odd numbered rows are K rows and read from right to left. Even numbered rows are P rows and read from left to right.
Use the Fair Isle method, strand the yarn not in use across the wrong side of work weaving it under and over the working yarn every 3 or 4 sts.

SIDES (both alike, make 2)
Using size 5 (3.75mm) needles and B cast on 55 sts.
Work entirely from Chart shaping as shown.
Bind off.

FINISHING
Using knitted pieces as templates and adding seam allowance, cut out front and back. Sew sides together between markers. Make lining in same way. Place lining inside bag, fold seam allowance to WS, and slip stitch lining in place along remainder of side seams and across bound-off edges.
Fold last 10 rows over handles and sew in place to inside of back and front.
Using D, make a pompom and sew to side of bag.

MAKING POMPOMS

You can buy a pompom maker, but if you don't have one, you can make your own very easily. Fold over a rectangle of card so that the folded card is the same diameter as the pompom you want to make. Cut a slit through the middle of the card and thread a piece of yarn at the folded end (to tie the center of the pompom). Then wrap the yarn for the pompom around the card until there is enough to make a full pompom. Tie the yarn around the center of the wrapped yarns at the middle of the card. Then cut the wrapped yarns at the top and bottom of the card. Slide the pompom off the card and trim it to shape.

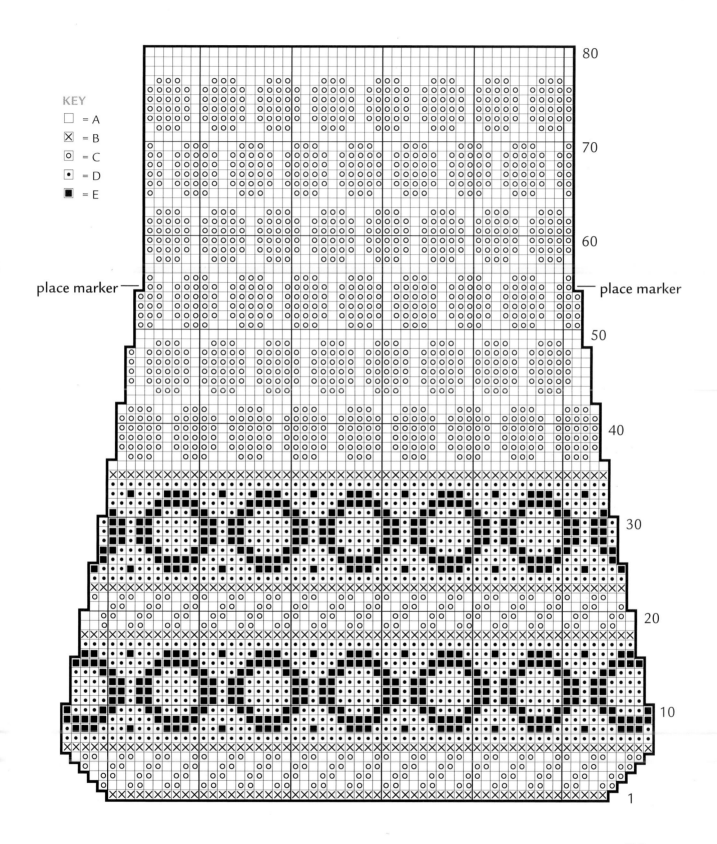

KEY

☐ = A
☒ = B
⊡ = C
⊙ = D
■ = E

place marker ——

—— place marker

80
70
60
50
40
30
20
10
1

NORDIC

This is a great traditional Scandinavian design, with its little reindeers alternating with hearts, in a classic dark red and beige colorway. The motifs here have been combined to create a cushion, but you could just as easily make a little crib blanket or use the designs on the pockets of a cardigan, for example. You can combine the Reindeer cushion with the Nordic Stripe cushion (see page 59) or you could use the Nordic stripe pattern as an alternative design on a patchwork blanket.

Reindeer Cushion

FINISHED SIZE
16¼in/41cm square

YARN
2 x 1¾oz/197yd balls of Rowan *Felted Tweed* in Rage 150 (A)
1 x 1¾oz/197yd ball of Rowan *Felted Tweed* in Clay 177 (B)

NEEDLES
Pair of size 3 (3.25mm) knitting needles
Pair of size 5 (3.75mm) knitting needles

EXTRAS
Six buttons, ⅝in/1.5cm diameter
16¼in/41cm cushion pad

GAUGE
23 sts and 32 rows to 4in/10cm square measured over St st using size 5 (3.75mm) needles *or size to obtain correct gauge.*

ABBREVIATIONS
See page 133.

NOTE
When working from Reindeer Chart, use the intarsia method (see page 130). Use a small separate ball of yarn for each area of color, twisting the yarns on wrong side when changing color to avoid a hole.
When working from Heart Chart, use the Fair Isle method (see page 131), stranding the yarn not in use across the wrong side of work weaving it under and over the working yarn every 3 or 4 sts.
When working from Chart, K rows read from right to left. P rows read from left to right.

Heart Square

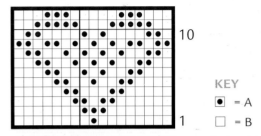

KEY
● = A
□ = B

Reindeer Square

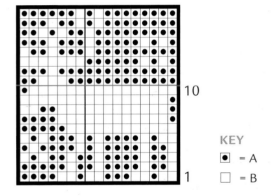

KEY
● = A
□ = B

REINDEER ALTERNATIVE

These little reindeer and heart designs would be perfect for a child's blanket. Make them up as you would the cushion motifs, but double the width and three times the length of the cushion, so you would need the cushion sample x 6 and to multiply up the yarn quantities x 5. You could add a matching garter stitch border to finish it off.

FRONT

Reindeer Square (make 5)

Using size 5 (3.75mm) needles and A cast on
31 sts.

Row 1 Using A, K to end.

Row 2 Using A, P to end.

Rows 3 to 13 Rep rows 1 and 2 five times more and
row 1 again.

Row 14 P7A, work across row 1 of Chart, P7A.

Row 15 K7A, work across row 2 of Chart, K7A.

Rows 16 to 31 Cont in this way to end of Chart.

Row 32 Using A, P to end.

Rows 33 to 44 Rep rows 1 and 2 six times.
Bind off.

Heart Square (make 4)

Using size 5 (3.75mm) needles and B cast on
31 sts.

Row 1 Using B, K to end.

Row 2 Using B, P to end.

Rows 3 to 16 Rep rows 1 and 2 seven times more.

Row 17 K7B, work across row 1 of Chart, K7B.

Row 18 P7B, work across row 2 of Chart, K7B.

Rows 19 to 28 Cont in this way to end of Chart.

Rows 29 to 44 Rep rows 1 and 2 eight times.
Bind off.

BACK

Lower Back

Using size 5 (3.75mm) needles and A cast on
95 sts.

Beg with a K row, work 60 rows in St st.
Change to size 3 (3.25mm) needles.

Row 1 K4, [P3, K3] to last 7 sts, P3, K4.

Row 2 P4, [K3, P3] to last 7 sts, K3, P4.

These 2 rows form rib.
Work a further 10 rows.
Bind off in rib.

Upper Back

Using size 3 (3.25mm) needles and A cast on
95 sts.

Row 1 K4, [P3, K3] to last 7 sts, P3, K4.

Row 2 P4, [K3, P3] to last 7 sts, K3, P4.

These 2 rows form rib.
Work a further 4 rows.

Buttonhole row Rib 9, [work 2 tog, yo, rib 13] 5
times, work 2 tog, yo, rib 9.

Work a further 5 rows.
Change to size 5 (3.75mm) needles.
Beg with a K row, work 60 rows in St st.
Bind off.

FINISHING

Front: Arrange the motifs to form one large square,
with a reindeer motif in each corner and the center.
Place the heart motifs on the center of each side.
Join seams (see page 133).

Back: Lap upper back rib over lower back rib and
baste in place.
With RS together, sew back to front. Turn to RS, sew
on buttons.
Insert cushion pad.

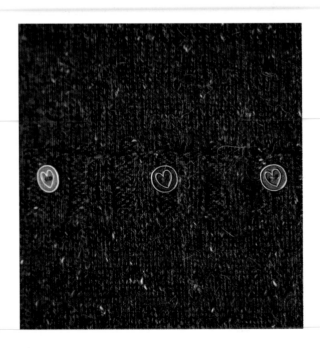

Stripe Cushion

FINISHED SIZE

16¼in/41cm square

YARN

2 x 1¾oz/197yd balls of Rowan *Felted Tweed* in Clay
177 (A)
1 x 1¾oz/197yd ball of Rowan *Felted Tweed* in Rage
150 (B)

NEEDLES

Pair of size 3 (3.25mm) knitting needles
Pair of size 5 (3.75mm) knitting needles

EXTRAS

Six buttons, ⅝in/1.5cm diameter
16¼in/41cm cushion pad

GAUGE

23 sts and 32 rows to 4in/10cm square measured
over St st using size 5 (3.75mm) needles *or size to
obtain correct gauge.*

ABBREVIATIONS

See page 133.

FRONT

Using size 5 (3.75mm) needles and A cast on
99 sts.
Row 1 Using A, K to end.
Row 2 Using A, P to end.
Row 3 Using A, K to end.
Row 4 Using A, P to end.
Row 5 K1A, [1B, 2A] to last 2 sts, 1B, 1A.
Row 6 Using A, P to end.
Row 7 Using A, K to end.
Row 8 Using B, P to end.
Row 9 Using B, K to end.

Row 10 P1B, [1A, 2B] to last 2 sts, 1A, 1B.
Row 11 Using B, K to end.
Row 12 Using B, P to end.
3rd to 12th rows form the stripe patt and are
repeated.
Rows 13 to 117 Rep rows 3 to 12 ten times more,
then rows 3 to 7 once.
Row 118 Using A, P to end.
Row 119 Using A, K to end.
Bind off.

BACK

Lower Back

Using size 5 (3.75mm) needles and A cast on
95 sts.
Beg with a K row, work 60 rows in St st.
Change to size 3 (3.25mm) needles.
Row 1 K4, [P3, K3] to last 7 sts, P3, K4.
Row 2 P4, [K3, P3] to last 7 sts, K3, P4.
These 2 rows form the rib.
Work a further 10 rows.
Bind off in rib.

Upper Back

Using size 3 (3.25mm) needles and A cast on
95 sts.
Row 1 K4, [P3, K3] to last 7 sts, P3, K4.
Row 2 P4, [K3, P3] to last 7 sts, K3, P4.
These 2 rows form the rib.
Work a further 4 rows.
Buttonhole row Rib 9, [work 2 tog, yo, rib 13]
5 times, work 2 tog, yo, rib 9.
Work a further 5 rows.
Change to size 5 (3.75mm) needles.
Beg with a K row, work 60 rows in St st.
Bind off.

FINISHING

Back: Lap upper back rib over lower back rib and
baste in place. With RS together, sew back to front.
Turn to RS, sew on buttons. Insert cushion pad.

KARI

This lacy heart design is typically Scandinavian and it is just right for this warm but light stole in an elegant silver colorway. The yarn is Rowan's Cashsoft 4-ply. We decided to make it with a seam at the back, so that the hearts run the same way at the front of the stole, but if this does not bother you, and the join does, you could knit it in one piece, so the hearts run the same way over the whole knitted piece.

FINISHED SIZE

17¾ x 63in/45 x 160cm (excluding edging)

YARN

9 x 1¾oz/197yd balls of Rowan *Cashsoft 4-ply* in Elite 451

NEEDLES

Pair of size 3 (3.25mm) knitting needles

GAUGE

28 sts and 36 rows to 4in/10cm square over patt using size 3 (3.25mm) needles *or size to obtain correct gauge.*

ABBREVIATIONS

See page 133.

STOLE (make 2 pieces)

Using size 3 (3.25mm) needles cast on 125 sts.

Row 1 (RS) With yarn at back, sl 1pw, K2, yo, K2tog, * K17, [yo, K2tog, K1] twice, yo, K2tog; rep from * 3 times more, K17, yo, K2tog, with yarn at back sl 1 pw.

Row 2 and every foll WS row P3, yo, P2tog, *P17, [yo, P2tog, P1] twice, yo, P2tog; rep from * 3 times more, P17, yo, P2tog, P1.

Row 3 With yarn at back, sl 1pw, K2, yo, K2tog, * K7, yo, skp, K8, [yo, K2tog, K1] twice, yo, K2tog; rep from * 3 times more, K7, yo, skp, K8, yo, K2tog, with yarn at back sl 1pw.

Row 5 With yarn at back, sl 1pw, K2, yo, K2tog, * K5, K2tog, yo, K1, yo, skp, K7, [yo, K2tog, K1], twice, yo, K2tog; rep from * 3 times more, K5, K2tog, yo, K1, yo, skp, K7, yo, K2tog, with yarn at back sl 1pw.

Row 7 With yarn at back, sl 1pw, K2, yo, K2tog, * K4, K2tog, yo, K3, yo, skp, K6, [yo, K2tog, K1] twice, yo, K2tog; rep from * 3 times more, K4, K2tog, yo, K3, yo, skp, K6, yo, K2tog, with yarn at back sl 1pw.

Row 9 With yarn at back, sl 1pw, K2, yo, K2tog, * K3, K2tog, yo, K5, yo, skp, K5, [yo, K2tog, K1] twice, yo, K2tog; rep from * 3 times more, K3, K2tog, yo, K5, yo, skp, K5, yo, K2tog, with yarn at back sl 1pw.

Row 11 With yarn at back, sl 1pw, K2, yo, K2tog, * K2, K2tog, yo, K7, yo, skp, K4, [yo, K2tog, K1] twice, yo, K2tog; rep from * 3 times more, K2, K2tog, yo, K7, yo, skp, K4, yo, K2tog, with yarn at back sl 1pw.

Row 13 With yarn at back, sl 1pw, K2, yo, K2tog, * K1, K2tog, yo, K4, [yo, skp, K3] twice, [yo, K2tog, K1] twice, yo, K2tog; rep from * 3 times more, K1, K2tog, yo, K4, [yo, skp, K3] twice, yo, K2tog, with yarn at back sl 1pw.

Row 15 With yarn at back, sl 1pw, K2, yo, K2tog, * K2, yo, skp, K1, K2tog, yo, K1, yo, skp, K1, K2tog, yo, K4, [yo, K2tog, K1] twice, yo, K2tog; rep from * 3 times more, K2, yo, skp, K1, K2tog, yo, K1, yo, skp, K1, K2tog, yo, K4, yo, K2tog, with yarn at back sl 1pw.

Row 17 With yarn at back, sl 1pw, K2, yo, K2tog, * K3, yo, sl 1, K2tog, psso, yo, K3, yo, s2kp, yo, K5, [yo, K2tog, K1] twice, yo, K2tog; rep from * 3 times more, K3, yo, sl 1, K2tog, psso, yo, K3, yo, s2kp, yo, K5, yo, K2tog, with yarn at back sl 1pw.

Row 18 P3, yo, P2tog, *P17, [yo, P2tog, P1] twice, yo, P2tog; rep from * 3 times more, P17, yo, P2tog, P1.

These 18 rows form the patt.

Rows 19 to 288 Rep rows 1 to 18 fifteen times more.

Leave these sts on a holder.

Joining row On one piece, slip sts from one needle to a spare needle. With RS together and both needles facing the same direction, [K one st together from each needle] twice, * take the first st over the needle, K one st together from each needle; rep from * to end of row. Fasten off.

EDGING

Using size 3 (3.25mm) needles cast on 6 sts.

Row 1 K2, yo, K2tog, yo, K2. *7 sts.*

Rows 2, 4, and 6 K to end.

Row 3 K2, yo, K2tog, K1, yo, K2. *8 sts.*

Row 5 K2, yo, K2tog, K2, yo, K2. *9 sts.*

Row 7 K2, yo, K2tog, K3, yo, K2. *10 sts.*

Row 8 Bind off 4 sts, K to end. *6 sts.*

These 8 rows form the patt.

Cont in patt until border fits round outside edge of Stole, ending with a row 8.

Bind off.

FINISHING

Sew edging in place, easing in round corners.

Join 6 bound-off sts to 6 cast-on sts.

HANS

This is a favorite and, fortunately, it fits me very well! I love the traditional Norwegian-style small all-over diamond pattern and the zigzag pattern at the bottom of the vest. One of the benefits of Fair Isle knitting is that the garment is double thickness—just what you need for a warm vest. It is knitted here in a subtle brown and cream color combination, but would look good in two tones of most colors.

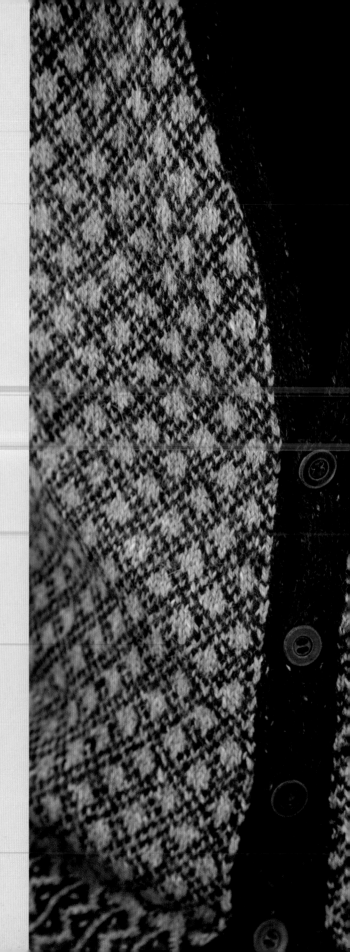

TO FIT CHEST

34–36	38–40	42–44	in
87–92	97–102	107–112	cm

FINISHED SIZE
Around chest

44½	48¾	53½	in
113	124	136	cm

Length to shoulder

24½	25¼	26	in
62	64	66	cm

YARN

4 (5: 5) x 1¾oz/197yd balls of Rowan *Felted Tweed* in Clay 177 (A)

3 (3: 3) x 1¾oz/197yd balls of Rowan *Felted Tweed* in Treacle 145 (B)

NEEDLES

Pair of size 3 (3.25mm) knitting needles
Pair of size 5 (3.75mm) knitting needles

EXTRAS

Five buttons, ¾in/17mm diameter

GAUGE

29 sts and 29 rows to 4in/10cm square over patt using size 5 (3.75mm) needles *or size to obtain correct gauge.*

ABBREVIATIONS

See page 133.

NOTE

When working from Chart, odd numbered rows are K rows and read from right to left. Even numbered rows are P rows and read from left to right.
Use the Fair Isle method, strand the yarn not in use across the wrong side of work weaving it under and over the working yarn every 3 or 4 sts.

BACK

With size 3 (3.25mm) needles and B, cast on 165 (181: 197) sts.

Row 1 Work first 3 sts, work across 8 st patt rep of row 1 20 (22: 24) times, work last 2 sts.

Row 2 Work first 2 sts, work across 8 st patt rep of row 2 20 (22: 24) times, work last 3 sts.

These 2 rows set the chart.

Cont to work in patt from Chart to end of row 20.

Change to size 5 (3.75mm) needles.

Cont in patt rep rows 21 to 28 only from Chart until work measures 15½ (15¾: 16¼)in/39 (40: 41)cm from cast-on edge, ending with a WS row.

Shape armholes

Bind off 10 sts at beg of next 2 rows.

145 (161: 177) sts.

Dec one st at each end of the next 7 (9: 11) rows then 5 foll right side rows, then 4 foll 4th rows.

113 (125: 137) sts.

Work even until back measures 24½ (25¼: 26)in/ 62 (64: 66)cm from cast-on edge, ending with a WS row.

Shape shoulders and back neck

Bind off 11 (12: 13) sts at beg of next 2 rows.

Next row Bind off 11 (12: 13) sts, patt until there are 15 (17: 19) sts on the needle, turn and work on these sts for first side of neck.

Next row Bind off 4 (5: 6) sts, patt to end.

Bind off rem 11 (12: 13) sts.

With RS facing, return to rem sts, rejoin yarn, bind off center 39 (43: 47) sts, patt to end.

Next row Bind off 11 (12: 13) sts patt to end.

Next row Bind off 4 (5: 6) sts, patt to end.

Bind off rem 11 (12: 13) sts.

LEFT FRONT

With size 3 (3.25mm) needles and B, cast on 83 (91: 99) sts.

Cont to work in patt from Chart to end of row 20.

Change to size 5 (3.75mm) needles.

Right front Left front Back

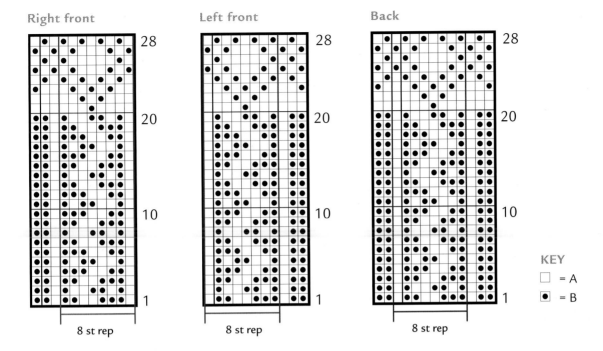

28 20 10 1

28 20 10 1

28 20 10 1

KEY

☐ = A

◉ = B

8 st rep 8 st rep 8 st rep

Cont in patt rep rows 21 to 28 only from Chart until work measures 15½ (15¾: 16¼)in/39 (40: 41)cm from cast-on edge, ending with a WS row.

Shape armhole and front neck

Next row Bind off 10 sts, patt to end.
73 (81: 89) sts.

Next row Patt to end.

Next row Work 2 tog, patt to last 2 sts, work 2 tog.

Next row Patt to last 2 sts, work 2 tog.

Rep the last 2 rows 2 (3: 4) times more and the first row again. *62 (67: 72) sts.*

Next row Patt to end.

Next row Work 2 tog, patt to last 2 sts, work 2 tog.

Rep the last 2 rows 4 more times. *52 (57: 62) sts.*

Next row Patt to end.

Next row Patt to last 2 sts, work 2 tog.

Next row Patt to end.

Next row Work 2 tog, patt to last 2 sts, work 2 tog.

Rep the last 4 rows 3 times more. *40 (45: 50) sts.*

Keeping armhole edge straight cont to dec at neck

edge on every 3rd row until 33 (36: 39) sts rem.

Work even until front measures the same as back to armhole shaping, ending at armhole edge.

Shape shoulder

Next row Bind off 11 (12: 13) sts at beg of next and foll right side row.

Work 1 row.

Bind off rem 11 (12: 13) sts.

RIGHT FRONT

With size 3 (3.25mm) needles and B, cast on 83 (91: 99) sts.

Cont to work in patt from Chart to end of row 20.

Change to size 5 (3.75mm) needles.

Cont in patt rep rows 21 to 28 only from Chart until work measures 15½ (15¾: 16¼)in/39 (40: 41)cm from cast-on edge, ending with a RS row.

Shape armhole and front neck

Next row Bind off 10 sts, patt to end.
73 (81: 89) sts.

73

Next row Work 2 tog, patt to last 2 sts, work 2 tog.

Next row Work 2 tog, patt to end.

Rep the last 2 rows 2 (3: 4) times more and the first row again. *62 (67: 72) sts.*

Next row Patt to end.

Next row Work 2 tog, patt to last 2 sts, work 2 tog.

Rep the last 2 rows 4 times more. *52 (57: 62) sts.*

Next row Patt to end.

Next row Work 2 tog, patt to end.

Next row Patt to end.

Next row Work 2 tog, patt to last 2 sts, work 2 tog.

Rep the last 4 rows 3 times more. *40 (45: 50) sts.*

Keeping armhole edge straight, cont to dec at neck edge on every 3rd row until 33 (36: 39) sts rem.

Work even until front measures the same as back to armhole shaping, ending at armhole edge.

Shape shoulder

Next row Bind off 11 (12: 13) sts at beg of next and foll WS row.

Work 1 row.

Bind off rem 11 (12: 13) sts.

BUTTONBAND

With size 3 (3.25mm) needles and B, cast on 9 sts.

Row 1 K2, [P1, K1] twice, P1, K2.

Row 2 K1, [P1, K1] to end.

Rep the last 2 rows until band, when slightly stretched, fits up right front and halfway round back neck, ending with row 1.

Bind off in rib.

Sew band in place.

Mark position for 5 buttons, the first ¾in/2cm from cast-on edge, the 5th ¾in/2cm below neck shaping, and the rem 3 spaced evenly between.

BUTTONHOLE BAND

With size 3 (3.25mm) needles and B, cast on 9 sts.

Row 1 K2, [P1, K1] twice, P1, K2.

Row 2 K1, [P1, K1] to end.

Rep the last 2 rows twice more.

Buttonhole row Rib 4, P2tog, yo, rib 3.

Cont in rib, working buttonholes to match markers, then work even until band, when slightly stretched, fits up left front and halfway round back neck, ending with row 1.

Bind off in rib.

Sew band in place.

ARMBANDS

Join shoulder seams.

With RS facing, using size 3 (3.25mm) needles and B, pick up and K128 (136: 144) sts evenly round armhole edge.

Rib row [K1, P1] to end.

Rep the last row 6 times more

Bind off in rib.

FINISHING

Join side and armband seams (see page 133).

Join bound-off edges of edging.

Sew on buttons.

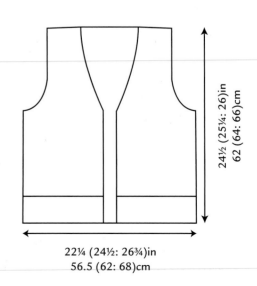

24½ (25¼: 26)in
62 (64: 66)cm

22¼ (24½: 26¾)in
56.5 (62: 68)cm

PIA

I have created two designs using a pretty twisted cable pattern, both of them knitted in soft, cozy Felted Tweed and ideal for keeping you warm in style. One is a snood, the other a pair of slouch socks. The snood is easier to knit as it involves no shaping and is simply a largish rectangle, ribbed at each end and with the sides stitched together. You can wear it over your head or like a cowl around your neck, as you prefer. For the socks, the cable stitch pattern is worked on the leg part of the sock alone, with a ribbed top and stockinette stitch for the shaped foot.

Pia Snood

FINISHED SIZE
Approx. length: 17in/43cm
Width (all round): 33½in/85cm

YARN
4 x 1¾oz/197yd balls of Rowan *Felted Tweed* in Scree 165

NEEDLES
Pair of size 3 (3.25mm) knitting needles
Pair of size 5 (3.75mm) knitting needles
Cable needle

GAUGE
23 sts and 32 rows to 4in/10cm square over St st using size 5 (3.75mm) needles *or size to obtain correct gauge.*
30sts and 32 rows to 4in/10cm square over cable patt using size 5 (3.75mm) needles *or size to obtain correct gauge.*

ABBREVIATIONS
See page 133.

SPECIAL ABBREVIATIONS
C4R = cross 4 right, slip next st on a cable needle and leave at back of work, K3, then P1 from cable needle; **C4L** = cross 4 left, slip next 3 sts on a cable needle and leave at front of work, P1, then K3 from cable needle.

Patt Panel A (worked over 16 sts)
Row 1 P4, C4R, C4L, P4.
Row 2 K4, P3, K2, P3, K4.
Row 3 P3, C4R, P2, C4L, P3.
Row 4 K3, P3, K4, P3, K3.
Row 5 P2, C4R, P4, C4L, P2.

Row 6 K2, P3, K6, P3, K2.
Row 7 P2, C4L, P4, C4R, P2.
Row 8 As row 4.
Row 9 P3, C4L, P2, C4R, P3.
Row 10 As row 2.
Row 11 P4, C4L, C4R, P4.
Row 12 K5, P6, K5.
These 12 rows form the patt panel.

Patt Panel B (worked over 12 sts)
Row 1 P3, C4R, P1, C4R.
Row 2 K1, P3, K2, P3, K3.
Row 3 P2, [C4R, P1] twice.
Row 4 K2, [P3, K2] twice.
Row 5 [P1, C4R] twice, P2.
Row 6 K3, P3, K2, P3, K1.
Row 7 C4R, P1, C4R, P3.
Row 8 K4, P3, K2, P3.
Row 9 C4L, P1, C4L, P3.
Row 10 As row 6.
Row 11 [P1, C4L] twice, P2.
Row 12 As row 4.
Row 13 P2, [C4L, P1] twice.
Row 14 As row 2.
Row 15 P3, C4L, P1, C4L.
Row 16 P3, K2, P3, K4.
These 16 rows form the patt panel.

Patt Panel C (worked over 12 sts)
Row 1 C4L, P1, C4L, P3.
Row 2 K3, P3, K2, P3, K1.
Row 3 [P1, C4L] twice, P2.
Row 4 K2, [P3, K2] twice.
Row 5 P2, [C4L, P1] twice.
Row 6 K1, P3, K2, P3, K3.
Row 7 P3, C4L, P1, C4L.
Row 8 P3, K2, P3, K4.

Row 9 P3, C4R, P1, C4R.
Row 10 As row 6.
Row 11 P2, [C4R, P1] twice.
Row 12 As row 4.
Row 13 [P1, C4R] twice, P2.
Row 14 As row 2.
Row 15 C4R, P1, C4R, P3.
Row 16 K4, P3, K2, P3.
These 16 rows form the patt panel.

BACK AND FRONT (both alike)
Using size 3 (3.25mm) needles cast on 128 sts.
Row 1 (RS) K3, [P2, K2] to last st, K1.
Row 2 P3, [K2, P2] to last st, P1.
These 2 rows form the rib.
Work a further 4 rows.
Change to size 5 (3.75mm) needles and patt.
Row 1 Work 1st row of Patt Panel A, [Patt Panel
B, Patt Panel A] twice, Patt Panel C, Patt Panel A]
twice.
Row 2 Work 2nd row of Patt Panel A, [Patt Panel
C, Patt Panel A] twice, [Patt Panel B, Patt Panel A]
twice.
These 2 rows set the position for the patt panels.
Work even until 128 rows have been worked in patt.
Change to size 3 (3.25mm) needles.
Row 1 (RS) K3, [P2, K2] to last st, K1.
Row 2 P3, [K2, P2] to last st, P1.
These 2 rows form the rib.
Work a further 4 rows.
Bind off in rib.

FINISHING
Join side seams (see page 133).

Pia Socks

FINISHED SIZE
To fit shoe size: US 6½–7½ (8½–9½)/UK 4–5 (6–7)
Length from base of heel: 9 (9½)in/23 (24)cm

YARN
2 x 1¾oz/197yd balls of Rowan *Felted Tweed* in
Scree 165

NEEDLES
Pair of size 3 (3.25mm) knitting needles
Pair of size 5 (3.75mm) knitting needles
Set of size 5 (3.75mm) double-pointed knitting
needles
Cable needle

GAUGE
23 sts and 32 rows to 4in/10cm square over St st
using size 5 (3.75mm) needles *or size to obtain correct
gauge.*

ABBREVIATIONS
See page 133.

SPECIAL ABBREVIATIONS
C4R = cross 4 right, slip next st on a cable needle
and leave at back of work, K3, then P1 from cable
needle; **C4L** = cross 4 left, slip next 3 sts on a cable
needle and leave at front of work, P1, then K3 from
cable needle; **wrap 1**= with yarn to front, slip next
st, turn, bring yarn to front, slip st back onto right
hand needle.

Patt Panel A (worked over 16 sts)
Row 1 P4, C4R, C4L, P4.
Row 2 K4, P3, K2, P3, K4.
Row 3 P3, C4R, P2, C4L, P3.
Row 4 K3, P3, K4, P3, K3.

Row 5 P2, C4R, P4, C4L, P2.
Row 6 K2, P3, K6, P3, K2.
Row 7 P2, C4L, P4, C4R, P2.
Row 8 As row 4.
Row 9 P3, C4L, P2, C4R, P3.
Row 10 As row 2.
Row 11 P4, C4L, C4R, P4.
Row 12 K5, P6, K5.
These 12 rows form the patt panel.

Patt Panel B (worked over 12 sts)
Row 1 P3, C4R, P1, C4R.
Row 2 K1, P3, K2, P3, K3.
Row 3 P2, [C4R, P1] twice.
Row 4 K2, [P3, K2] twice.
Row 5 [P1, C4R] twice, P2.
Row 6 K3, P3, K2, P3, K1.
Row 7 C4R, P1, C4R, P3.
Row 8 K4, P3, K2, P3.
Row 9 C4L, P1, C4L, P3.
Row 10 As row 6.
Row 11 [P1, C4L] twice, P2.
Row 12 As row 4.
Row 13 P2, [C4L, P1] twice.
Row 14 As row 2.
Row 15 P3, C4L, P1, C4L.
Row 16 P3, K2, P3, K4.
These 16 rows form the patt panel.

Patt Panel C (worked over 12 sts)
Row 1 C4L, P1, C4L, P3.
Row 2 K3, P3, K2, P3, K1.
Row 3 [P1, C4L] twice, P2.
Row 4 K2, [P3, K2] twice.
Row 5 P2, [C4L, P1] twice.
Row 6 K1, P3, K2, P3, K3.
Row 7 P3, C4L, P1, C4L.

Row 8 P3, K2, P3, K4.

Row 9 P3, C4R, P1, C4R.

Row 10 As row 6.

Row 11 P2, [C4R, P1] twice.

Row 12 As row 4.

Row 13 [P1, C4R] twice, P2.

Row 14 As row 2.

Row 15 C4R, P1, C4R, P3.

Row 16 K4, P3, K2, P3.

These 16 rows form the patt panel.

SOCKS (make 2)

Using size 3 (3.25mm) needles cast on 72 sts.

Row 1 (RS) K3, [P2, K2] to last st, K1.

Row 2 P3, [K2, P2] to last st, P1.

These 2 rows form the rib.

Work a further 4 rows.

Change to size 5 (3.75mm) needles and patt.

Row 1 Work 1st row of Patt Panel A, Patt Panel B, Patt Panel A, Patt Panel C, Patt Panel A.

Row 2 Work 2nd row of Patt Panel A, Patt Panel C, Patt Panel A, Patt Panel B, Patt Panel A.

These 2 rows set the position for the patt panels.

Work even until 48 rows have been worked in patt.

Dec row [K2tog, K1, K2tog, K2] 10 times, K2tog. *51 sts.*

Next row P to end.

Cut yarn.

Cont on double-pointed needles and St st.

Shape heel

Slip next 13 sts on first needle, next 13 sts on second needle, next 13 sts on third needle and last 12 sts on end of first needle.

Rejoin yarn to beg of first needle.

Next row K24, wrap 1.

Next row P23, wrap 1.

Next row K22, wrap 1.

Next row P21, wrap 1.

Cont in this way, working one less st on every row until the foll row has been worked:

Next row P11, wrap 1.

Next row K11, wrap 1.

Next row P12, wrap 1.

Cont in this way, working one more st on every row until the foll row has been worked:

Next row K23, wrap 1.

Next row P24, wrap first st on next needle.

With RS facing, slip next 17 sts on first needle, next 17 sts on second needle, and next 17 sts on third needle.

Cont in rounds of St st until sock measures 5½ (6) in/14 (15)cm from last dec row, dec one st at end of last round. *50 sts.*

Shape toe

Next round [K1, skp, K19, K2tog, K1] twice.

Next round K to end.

Next round [K1, skp, K17, K2tog, K1] twice.

Next round K to end.

Next round [K1, skp, K15, K2tog, K1] twice.

Next round K to end.

Cont in rounds dec on every alt round as set until the foll round has been worked.

Next round [K1, skp, K7, K2tog, K1] twice.

Slip first 11 sts onto one needle and rem 11 sts onto a second needle.

Fold sock inside out and bind one st from each needle off together.

ADAPTING THE DESIGN

These socks are designed as "slouch" socks so that they slightly ruche on the leg and are not too tight around the ribbed top. If you want to wear them as ordinary socks, then you could increase the length of the rib by an inch or so, and possibly knit the rib as a K1, P1 rib rather than the K2, P2 rib shown here. Alternatively, reduce the needle size further for the rib to make it slightly tighter.

LIV

This big poncho-style cover-up
has some really chunky cable
detailing on the front and back,
but otherwise it is a simple shape
to knit—basically a big rectangle
with a ribbed cowl neck and cuffs,
and wide garter stitch borders.
On a very windy, cold day, it kept
Nathalie warm as toast. It is
knitted in really thick, soft Rowan
Felted Tweed Aran, so despite
being big, it knits up very fast.

FINISHED SIZE
Wrist to wrist: 61½in/156cm, with cuffs turned back
Length: 25¼in/64cm

YARN
24 x 1¾oz/197yd balls of Rowan *Felted Tweed Aran* in
Soot 729

NEEDLES
Pair of size 7 (4.5mm) knitting needles
Circular size 8 (5mm) knitting needle
Circular size 7 (4.5mm) knitting needle
Cable needle

GAUGE
16 sts and 23 rows to 4in/10cm square measured
over St st using size 8 (5mm) needles *or size to obtain
correct gauge.*

ABBREVIATIONS
See page 133.

SPECIAL ABBREVIATIONS
C8B = cable 8 back, slip next 4 sts on a cable needle
and leave at back of work, K4, then K4 from cable
needle; **C8F** = cable 8 front, slip next 4 sts on a cable
needle and leave at front of work, K4, then K4 from
cable needle.

BACK
Using size 7 (4.5mm) circular needle cast on
212 sts.
K 12 rows.
Row 13 K8, leave these sts on a holder for left back
border, K84, * M1, K4, M1, K3, M1, K2, M1, K4,
M1 *, K2, rep from * to * once, K to last 8 sts, leave
these 8 sts on a holder for right back border. *206 sts.*
Change to size 8 (5mm) circular needle.
Row 1 (RS) K82, [P2, K18] twice, P2, K82.
Row 2 P82, [K2, P8] 4 times, K2, P82.
Rows 3 and 4 As rows 1 and 2.

Row 5 K82, [P2, C8F, P2, C8B] twice, P2, K82.
Row 6 P82, [K2, P4, K10, P4] twice, K2, P82.
Row 7 K82, [P2, K4, P10, K4] twice, P2, K82.
Row 8 As row 6.
Rows 9 to 16 Rep rows 1 and 2 four times.
These 16 rows form the patt.
Work a further 98 rows.
Place a marker at each end of last row.
Work a further 22 rows.
Shape back neck and shoulder
Next row Patt 83, turn.
Next row P2tog, P to end.
Leave these 82 sts on a spare needle.
With right side facing rejoin yarn to rem sts, bind off
40 sts, patt to end.
Next row P to last 2 sts, P2tog.
Leave these 82 sts on a spare needle.

FRONT
Work as given for Back until 108 rows have been
worked.
Shape front neck
Next row Patt 90, K2tog, turn and work on
these sts.
Next row P2tog, patt to end.
Next row Patt to last 2 sts, K2tog.
Next row P2tog, patt to end.
Next row Patt to end.
Rep the last 2 rows twice more.
Next row P2tog, patt to end.
Patt 3 rows.
Rep the last 4 rows twice and the first row again.
82 sts.
Patt 8 rows.
Leave these sts on a spare needle.
With RS facing, rejoin yarn to rem sts, bind off
center 22 sts, skp, patt to end.
Complete to match first side, reversing shapings,
working P2tog tbl instead of P2tog.
Place a marker 24 rows down from each shoulder to
match markers on back.

COLLAR

With wrong sides of back and front together, join shoulder seams by knitting one st together from each needle and binding off in the usual way.

With RS facing, starting at left shoulder, using size 7 (4.5mm) circular needle, pick up and K31 sts down left side of front neck, 22 sts from center front, 31 sts up right side of front neck, and 40 sts from back neck. *124 sts.*

Round 1 [K2, P2] to end.

Rep the last round for 4in/10cm.

Next round [K1, M1, K1, P2] to end of round.

Change to size 8 (5mm) circular needle.

Next round [K3, P2] to end of round.

Rep the last round for 4in/10cm.

Bind off in rib.

CUFFS

With RS facing, using size 7 (4.5mm) needles pick up and K42 sts between markers.

Row 1 K2, [P2, K2] to end.

Row 2 P2, [K2, P2] to end.

Rep the last 2 rows for 9½in/24cm, ending with row 1.

Bind off in rib.

RIGHT FRONT AND LEFT BACK BORDER

With RS facing, using size 7 (4.5mm) needles, return to sts on holder, inc in first st, then K rem 7 sts. *9 sts.*

Cont in garter st until border, when slightly stretched, fits up left side of work to shoulder, ending with a WS row.

Leave sts on a holder.

LEFT FRONT AND RIGHT BACK BORDER

With WS facing, using size 7 (4.5mm) needles, return to sts on holder, inc in first st, then K rem 7 sts. *9 sts.*

Cont in garter st until border, when slightly stretched, fits up RS of work to shoulder, ending with a WS row.

Leave sts on a holder.

FINISHING

Graft border sts together to match shoulder seams (see page 133). Join cuff seams, reversing seam for 5in/13cm for turn back. Sew on borders.

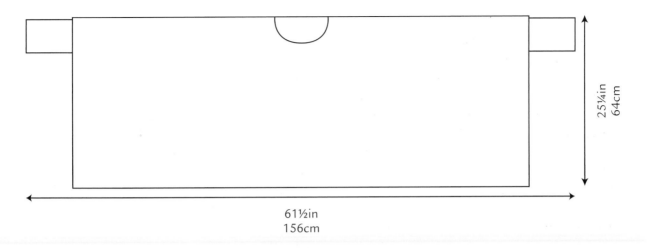

25¼in
64cm

61½in
156cm

HENDRIK

This bag is unisex—it works just as well for guys or girls. The snowflake design on the flap is a traditional Scandinavian pattern, often knitted in black and white, but I softened it here to shades of gray for a more contemporary, minimalist look. If you line the gusset with a piece of card (enclosed in a fabric envelope), it will give the base of the bag more strength and prevent it from flopping with heavier items in the bag. The handle and gusset are knitted all in one. The bag is lined in cotton. Pick a matching stripe or geometric design that suits the style of the bag.

FINISHED SIZE

Approx. 16¼ x 11in/41 x 28cm

YARN

2 x 1¾oz/197yd balls of Rowan *Felted Tweed* in Scree 165 (A)
3 x 1¾oz/197yd balls of Rowan *Felted Tweed* in Carbon 159 (B)

NEEDLES

Pair of size 3 (3.25mm) knitting needles
Pair of size 5 (3.75mm) knitting needles

EXTRAS

49¼in/125cm of 2in/5cm wide petersham ribbon
Lining fabric, 19½in x 1⅛yd/50cm x 1m
Microfiber batting (⅛in/3mm thick), 19½in x 1⅛yd/50cm x 1m
Cardboard for base of bag

GAUGE

23 sts and 29 rows to 4in/10cm square measured over dotted stripe patt using size 5 (3.75mm) needles *or size to obtain correct gauge.*
25 sts and 26 rows to 4in/10cm square measured over snowflake patt using size 5 (3.75mm) needles *or size to obtain correct gauge.*

ABBREVIATIONS

See page 133.

NOTE

When working from Chart, odd numbered rows are K rows and read from right to left. Even numbered rows are P rows and read from left to right.
Use the Fair Isle method, strand the yarn not in use across the wrong side of work weaving it under and over the working yarn every 3 or 4 sts.

FRONT

Using size 5 (3.75mm) needles and B cast on 85 sts.
Row 1 Using B, K to end.
Row 2 Using B, inc in first st, P to last 2 sts, inc in next st, P1.
Row 3 Using B, inc in first st, K[1A, 2B] to last 2 sts, K1A, using B, inc in last st.
Row 4 Using B, inc in first st, P to last 2 sts, inc in next st, P1.
Row 5 Using B, inc in first st, K to last 2 sts, inc in next st, K1.
Row 6 Using A, inc in first st, P to last 2 sts, inc in next st, P1. *95 sts.*
Row 7 Using A, K to end.
Row 8 P2A, [1B, 2A] to end.
Row 9 Using A, K to end.
Row 10 Using A, P to end.
Row 11 Using B, K to end.
Row 12 Using B, P to end.
Row 13 K2B, [1A, 2B] to end.
Row 14 Using B, P to end.
Row 15 Using B, K to end.
Row 16 Using A, P to end.
Rows 7 to 16 form the stripe patt and are repeated.
Rows 17 to 80 Rep rows 7 to 16 rows 6 times more, then rows 7 to 10 once **. Bind off.

BACK

Work as Front to **.
Mark each end of last row with a colored thread.
Row 81 Using B, skp, K to last 2 sts, K2tog. *93 sts.*
Row 82 Using B, K1, P1, K1, P to last 3 sts, K1, P1, K1.
Row 83 Using B, K1, P1, K2, K[1A, 2B] to last 2 sts, using B, P1, K1.
Row 84 As row 82.
Row 85 Using B, K1, P1, K to last 2 sts, P1, K1.
Row 86 Using B, K1, P1, K1, using A, P to last 3 sts, using B, K1, P1, K1.

Row 87 Using B, K1, P1, K1, using A K to last 3 sts, using B, K1, P1, K1.

Row 88 Using B, K1, P1, K1, P1A, [1B, 2A] to last 4 sts, 1A, using B, K1, P1, K1.

Row 89 As row 87.

Row 90 As row 86.

Row 91 Using B, K1, P1, K to last 2 sts, P1, K1.

Rows 92 to 129 Rep rows 82 to 91 three times more, then rows 82 to 89 once.

Row 130 (inc) Using B, K1, P1, K1, using A, P8, M1, [P10, M1] 7 times, P9, using B, K1, P1, K1. *101 sts.*

Row 131 Using B, K1, P1, K to last 2 sts, P1, K1.

Row 132 Using B, K1, P1, K1, P to last 3 sts, K1, P1, K1.

Row 133 Using B, K1, P1, K1, K across 13 st patt rep of row 1 of Chart seven times, then K 4 edge sts, using B, K1, P1, K1.

Row 134 Using B, K1, P1, K1, P 4 edge sts, then P 13 st patt rep of row 2 of Chart seven times, using B, K1, P1, K1.

Rows 135 to 151 Cont in this way to end of Chart.

Row 152 Using B, K1, P1, K1, P to last 3 sts, K1, P1, K1.

Row 153 Using B, K1, P1, K7, [K2tog, K7] 9 times, K2tog, K7, P1, K1. *91 sts.*

Change to size 3 (3.25mm) needles.

Row 154 Using B, K1, [P1, K1] to end.

Rows 155 to 157 As row 154.

Bind off in seed st.

GUSSET AND HANDLE

Gusset

Using size 5 (3.75mm) needles and B cast on 12 sts.

Beg with a K row, cont in St st until work—unstretched—fits from bound-off edge on front along row ends, cast-on edge, and row ends to bound-off edge, ending with a P row.

Mark each end of last row with a colored thread.

Handle

Cast on 7 sts at beg of next 2 rows.

Next row K6, sl 1pw, K12, sl 1pw, K6.

Next row P to end.

Rep the last 2 rows until strip measures 49¼in/ 125cm from colored threads.

Bind off.

FINISHING

Using knitted pieces as a templates and adding seam allowance, cut out front, back, and flap and gusset pieces from lining and batting. Baste batting to lining and use as one piece.

Join center 12 sts of bound-off edge of handle to cast-on edge of gusset. Sew row ends of gusset to row ends and cast-on edges of back and front. Make up lining in same way. Place lining inside bag, fold seam allowance to WS, and slip stitch lining in place, sewing flap lining inside seed st borders. Place petersham ribbon along center of WS of handle and slip stitch in place along knitted slipped sts. Bring row ends of handle together encasing petersham ribbon and sew row ends together to form seam. For extra stiffness in bottom of bag, cut a piece of cardboard to fit bottom. From lining make a "bag" to fit cardboard. Place in bottom of bag.

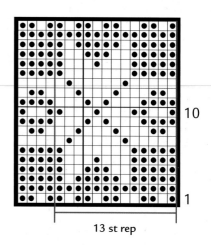

13 st rep

KEY

☐ = A

⊡ = B

DIXIE

These little mugwarmers are a fun project if, like me, you drink a lot of tea or coffee. They do the trick of keeping your drinks warm, too. They are ideal for practising Fair Isle knitting for the first time, as they are just rows of straight ribbing, using only two toning colors. The button is fastened with a button loop rather than a buttonhole, so you don't even have to worry about that either! They are knitted in Rowan Cocoon, which knits up quickly too. The yarn quantity in the pattern will make up two mugwarmers—just reverse the color key to make the alternative colorway.

FINISHED SIZE

To fit mug with 9½in/24cm circumference

YARN

1 x 1¾oz/197yd ball each of Rowan *Cocoon* in Crag 809 (A) and Fog 820 (B)

NEEDLES

Pair of size 10½ (7mm) knitting needles

EXTRAS

One button for each mug, ¾in/2cm diameter
Mug with 9½in/24cm circumference

GAUGE

15 sts and18 rows to 4in/10cm square measured over Fair Isle St st using size 10½ (7mm) needles *or size to obtain correct gauge.*

ABBREVIATIONS

See page 133.

MUGWARMER

Using size 10½ (7mm) needles and A cast on 37 sts.
Row 1 (RS) Using A, K1, [P1, K1] to end.
Row 2 Using A, P1, [K1, P1] to end.
Row 3 Using A, K to end.
Using **Fair Isle** technique, cont as folls:
Row 4 P [1A, 1B] to last st, 1A.
Place markers at both ends of last row.
Row 5 Using A, K to end.
Row 6 Using A, P to end.
Row 7 K1A, [1A, 1B] to last 2 sts, 2A.
Row 8 Using A, P to end.
Row 9 Using A, K to end.
Row 10 P [1A, 1B] to last st, 1A.
Row 11 Using A, K to end.
Row 12 (WS) Using A, P1, [K1, P1] to end.
Row 13 Using A, K1 ,[P1, K1] to end.
Bind off ribwise.

FINISHING

Join row-ends of mugwarmer from markers down to cast-on edge only.
Make a button loop to fit a ¾in/2cm button on upper edge of mugwarmer.
Sew button to opposite edge in order to correspond with button loop and placing center of button approx ⅝in/1.5cm in from row-end edge.
Slip warmer onto mug (cast-on edge to lower edge of mug) and button just under top of mug handle to secure.

MAKING A TWISTED CORD

You can make a twisted cord for the button loops by twisting the two colors of yarn together. Tie the two yarns to a door handle and tie a pencil to the other two ends. Then twist the pencil over and over, so that the yarns twist together, keeping the yarn taut as you twist. Then tie a knot at each end.

SNOWFLAKE

This traditional Scandinavian snowflake pattern works really well on these simple knitted placemats, coasters, and table runner. I chose to use Rowan Felted Tweed in two colors—brown and cream—and made some of the placemats and coasters in brown with a cream snowflake, and others in cream with a brown one. A simple seed stitch edging keeps the placemats, coasters, and runner flat, so that the edges do not curl.

Snowflake Runner

FINISHED SIZE
11¾ x 59in/30 x 150cm

YARN
4 x 1¾oz/197yd balls of Rowan *Felted Tweed* in Treacle 145 (A)

1 x 1¾oz/197yd ball of Rowan *Felted Tweed* in Clay 177 (B)

NEEDLES
Pair of size 5 (3.75mm) knitting needles

GAUGE
23 sts and 32 rows to 4in/10cm square measured over St st using size 5 (3.75mm) needles *or size to obtain correct gauge.*

ABBREVIATIONS
See page 133.

NOTE
When working from Chart, K rows are read from right to left. P rows are read from left to right. Use the Fair Isle method, strand the yarn not in use across the wrong side of work weaving it under and over the working yarn every 3 or 4 sts.

RUNNER
Using size 5 (3.75mm) needles and A cast on 69 sts.

Row 1 K1, [P1, K1] to end.

This row forms the seed st.

Work a further 7 rows.

Row 9 [K1, P1] twice, K to last 4 sts, [P1, K1] twice.

Row 10 K1, [P1, K1] twice, P to last 5 sts, [K1, P1] twice, K1.

Rows 11 to 30 Rep the last 2 rows 10 times more.

KEY □ = A ☒ = B

SNOWFLAKE ALTERNATIVE

The snowflake design worked at either end of this placemat would make an attractive design for a patchwork cushion, too. You could alternate the snowflake with plain knit patches to the same size or create simple stripes in the two colorways used in the snowflake. If you make it up in the dark red and soft beige used for the cushions on page 116, it would add to an attractive set.

Row 31 [K1, P1] twice, K17, work across row 1 of Chart, K17, [P1, K1] twice.

Row 32 K1, [P1, K1] twice, P16, work across row 2 of Chart, P16, [K1, P1] twice, K1.

These 2 rows set the position for the motif.

Rows 33 to 57 Cont in this way to end of chart.

Row 58 K1, [P1, K1] twice, P to last 5 sts, [K1, P1] twice, K1.

Row 59 [K1, P1] twice, K to last 4 sts, [P1, K1] twice.

Rep the last 2 rows 183 times more.

Row 426 K1, [P1, K1] twice, P16, work across row 1 of Chart, P16, [K1, P1] twice, K1.

Row 427 [K1, P1] twice, K17, work across row 2 of Chart, K17, [P1, K1] twice.

These 2 rows set the position for the motif.

Rows 428 to 452 Cont in this way to end of chart.

Row 453 [K1, P1] twice, K to last 4 sts, [P1, K1] twice.

Row 456 K1, [P1, K1] twice, P to last 5 sts, [K1, P1] twice, K1.

Rows 457 to 476 Rep the last 2 rows 10 times more.

Row 477 K1, [P1, K1] to end.

Rep the last row 7 times more.

Bind off in seed st.

Snowflake Placemat

FINISHED SIZE
15¾ x 11¾in/40 x 30cm

YARN
1st colorway
1 x 1¾oz/197yd ball of Rowan *Felted Tweed* in Treacle 145 (A)
1 x 1¾oz/197yd ball of Rowan *Felted Tweed* in Clay 177 (B)
2nd colorway
1 x 1¾oz/197yd ball of Rowan *Felted Tweed* in Clay 177 (A)
1 x 1¾oz/197yd ball of Rowan *Felted Tweed* in Treacle 145 (B)

NEEDLES
Pair of size 5 (3.75mm) knitting needles

GAUGE
23 sts and 32 rows to 4in/10cm square measured over St st using size 5 (3.75mm) needles *or size to obtain correct gauge.*

ABBREVIATIONS
See page 133.

NOTE
When working from Chart, odd numbered rows are K rows and read from right to left. Even numbered rows are P rows and read from left to right.
Use the Fair Isle method, strand the yarn not in use across the wrong side of work weaving it under and over the working yarn every 3 or 4 sts.

PLACEMAT
Using size 5 (3.75mm) needles and A cast on 91 sts.

Row 1 K1, [P1, K1] to end.
This row forms the seed st.
Work a further 7 rows.
Row 9 [K1, P1] twice, K to last 4 sts, [P1, K1] twice.
Row 10 K1, [P1, K1] twice, P to last 5 sts, [K1, P1] twice, K1.
Rows 11 to 34 Rep the last 2 rows 12 times more.
Row 35 [K1, P1] twice, K28, work across row 1 of Chart, K28, [P1, K1] twice.
Row 36 K1, [P1, K1] twice, P27, work across row 2 of Chart, P27, [K1, P1] twice, K1.
These 2 rows set the position for the motif.
Rows 37 to 61 Cont in this way to end of chart.
Row 62 As row 10.
Row 63 As row 9.
Rows 64 to 87 Rep the last 2 rows 12 times more.
Row 88 K1, [P1, K1] to end.
Rows 89 to 95 Rep the last row 7 times more.
Bind off in seed st.

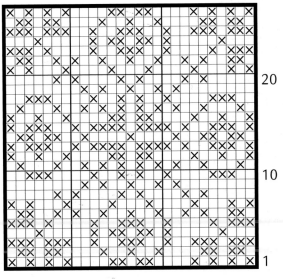

KEY ☐ = A ☒ = B

Snowflake Coasters

FINISHED SIZE
6¾ x 5½in/17.5x 14cm

YARN
1st colorway
1 x 1¾oz/197yd ball of Rowan *Felted Tweed* in Treacle 145 (A)
1 x 1¾oz/197yd ball of Rowan *Felted Tweed* in Clay 177 (B)
2nd colorway
1 x 1¾oz/197yd ball of Rowan *Felted Tweed* in Clay 177 (A)
1 x 1¾oz/197yd ball of Rowan *Felted Tweed* in Treacle 145 (B)

NEEDLES
Pair of size 5 (3.75mm) knitting needles

GAUGE
23 sts and 32 rows to 4in/10cm square measured over St st using size 5 (3.75mm) needles *or size to obtain correct gauge.*

ABBREVIATIONS
See page 133.

NOTE
When working from Chart, odd numbered rows are K rows and read from right to left. Even numbered rows are P rows and read from left to right.
Use the Fair Isle method, strand the yarn not in use across the wrong side of work weaving it under and over the working yarn every 3 or 4 sts.

COASTER
Using size 5 (3.75mm) needles and A cast on 41 sts.

Row 1 K1, [P1, K1] to end.
This row forms the seed st.
Work a further 3 rows.
Row 5 K1, P1, K to last 2 sts, P1, K1.
Row 6 K1, P1, K1, P to last 3 sts, K1, P1, K1.
Rows 7 and 8 Rep rows 5 and 6 once more.
Row 9 K1, P1, K5, work across row 1 of Chart, K5, P1, K1.
Row 10 K1, P1, K1, P4, work across row 2 of Chart, P4, K1, P1, K1.
These 2 rows set the position for the motif.
Rows 11 to 35 Cont in this way to end of chart.
Row 36 K1, P1, K1, P to last 3 sts, K1, P1, K1.
Row 37 K1, P1, K to last 2 sts, P1, K1.
Rows 38 and 39 Rep rows 36 and 37 once more.
Row 40 K1, [P1, K1] to end.
Rep the last row 3 times more.
Bind off in seed st.

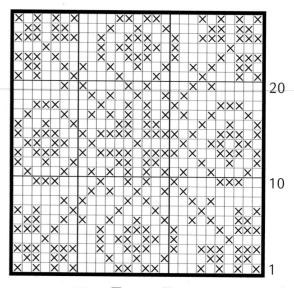

KEY ☐ = A ☒ = B

PEPPI

This is another traditional Fair Isle pattern, but with an injection of more contemporary colors and using fewer of them than the Astrid Fair Isle designs—just five. The socks are slipper socks, with a defined sole. The cushion employs the same Fair Isle design and colorways as the socks but places the pattern in two bands across the center of the cushion. They are all knitted in Rowan Felted Tweed (as are the Nordic Cushions, on page 54). You can, if you wish, add this cushion to the Nordic cushions to make a set.

Peppi Socks

FINISHED SIZE
To fit shoe size: US 6½–7½ (7½–8½)/UK 4–5 (5–6)
Length from base of heel: 10½ (11)in/26.5 (28)cm

YARN
2 x 1¾oz/197yd balls of Rowan *Felted Tweed* in Rage
150 (M)
1 x 1¾oz/197yd ball each of Rowan *Felted Tweed* in
Avocado 161 (A), Melody 142 (B), Clay 177 (C),
Treacle 145 (D), and Gilt 160 (E)

NEEDLES
Pair of size 3 (3.25mm) knitting needles
Pair of size 5 (3.75mm) knitting needles
Circular size 5 (3.75mm) needle

GAUGE
30 sts and 28 rows to 4in/10cm square measured
over patterned St st using size 5 (3.75mm) needles
or size to obtain correct gauge.

ABBREVIATIONS
See page 133.

NOTE
When working from Chart, odd numbered rows are
K rows and read from right to left. Even numbered
rows are P rows and read from left to right.
Use the Fair Isle method, strand the yarn not in use
across the wrong side of work weaving it under and
over the working yarn every 3 or 4 sts.

SLIPPER SOCKS (make 2)
Using size 3 (3.25mm) needles and A cast on
70 sts.
Row 1 (RS) K2, [P2, K2] to end.
Row 2 P2, [K2, P2] to end.

These 2 rows form the rib.

Work a further 8 rows, inc 5 sts evenly across last row. *75 sts.*

Change to size 5 (3.75mm) needles.

Cont in patt from Chart.

Row 1 Work first st, work across 12 st patt rep of row 1 six times, work last 2 sts.

Row 2 Work first 2 sts, work across 12 st patt rep of row 2 six times, work last st.

These 2 rows set the chart.

Cont in patt to end of Chart.

Cont in M only.

Next row P3, [P2tog, P4] 12 times. *63 sts.*

Cont in St st until work measures 8¼in/21cm from cast-on edge, ending with a P row.

Shape instep

Next row K21, leave these sts on a holder, K21, turn, place rem 21 sts on a holder.

Cont in St st and work 5½ (6¼)in/14 (16)cm on these center 21 sts, ending with a P row.

Next row K1, skp, K to last 3 sts, K2tog, K1.

Next row P1, P2tog, P to last 3 sts, P2tog tbl, P1.

Rep the last 2 rows once more. *13 sts.*

Cut off yarn.

With RS facing, using size 5 (3.75mm) circular needle, slip first set of 21 sts on needle, rejoin yarn at base of instep and pick up and K34 (38) sts along side of instep, K center 13 sts then pick up and K34 (38) sts along other side of instep, K21 from holder. *123 (131) sts.*

Beg with a P row, work 9 rows in St st.

Break off yarn.

Shape sole

Next row Slip first 54 (58) sts onto right-hand needle, rejoin yarn and K15 sts, turn.

Next row K16, turn.

Next row K17, turn.

Next row K18, turn.

Next row K19, turn.

Next row K18, K2tog, turn.

Rep last row until 37 sts rem.

Next row K17, s2kp, turn.

Next row K16, s2kp, turn.

Next row K15, s2kp, turn.

Next row K14, s2kp, turn.

Next row K to end.

Bind off.

FINISHING

Join back seam (see page 133). With back seam to center of bound-off, join heel seam.

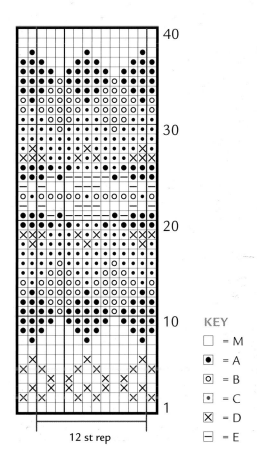

40

30

20

10

1

KEY

☐ = M

● = A

⊙ = B

⊡ = C

☒ = D

⊟ = E

12 st rep

Peppi Cushion

FINISHED SIZE
16¼in/41cm square

YARN
3 x 1¾oz/197yd balls of Rowan *Felted Tweed* in Rage 150 (M)
1 x 1¾oz/197yd ball of Rowan *Felted Tweed* each in Avocado 161 (A), Melody 142 (B), Clay 177 (C), Treacle 145 (D), and Gilt 160 (E)

NEEDLES
Pair of size 3 (3.25mm) knitting needles
Pair of size 5 (3.75mm) knitting needles

EXTRAS
Six buttons, ⅝in/1.5cm diameter
16¼in/41cm cushion pad

GAUGE
23 sts and 32 rows to 4in/10cm square measured over St st using size 5 (3.75mm) needles *or size to obtain correct gauge.*

ABBREVIATIONS
See page 133.

NOTE
When working from Chart, odd numbered rows are K rows and read from right to left. Even numbered rows are P rows and read from left to right.
Use the Fair Isle method, strand the yarn not in use across the wrong side of work weaving it under and over the working yarn every 3 or 4 sts.

FRONT
Using size 5 (3.75mm) needles and A cast on 95 sts.

Beg with a K row work 25 rows in St st.
Next row (inc) P7, m1pw, [P3, m1pw] 27 times, P7. *123 sts.*
Cont in patt from Chart.
Row 1 Work first st, work across 12 st patt rep of row 1 ten times, work last 2 sts.
Row 2 Work first 2 sts, work across 12 st patt rep of row 2 ten times, work last st.
These 2 rows set the chart.
Cont in patt to end of row 38, then work rows 1 to 31 again.
Cont in M only.
Next row P7, P2tog, [P2, P2tog] 27 times, P6. *95 sts.*
Beg with a K row work 25 rows in St st.
Bind off.

BACK
Lower Back
Using size 5 (3.75mm) needles and A cast on 95 sts.
Beg with a K row, work 60 rows in St st.
Change to size 3 (3.25mm) needles.
Row 1 K4, [P3, K3] to last 7 sts, P3, K4.
Row 2 P4, [K3, P3] to last 7 sts, K3, P4.
These 2 rows form the rib.
Work a further 10 rows.
Bind off in rib.
Upper Back
Using size 3 (3.25mm) needles and A cast on 95 sts.
Row 1 K4, [P3, K3] to last 7 sts, P3, K4.
Row 2 P4, [K3, P3] to last 7 sts, K3, P4.
These 2 rows form the rib.
Work a further 4 rows.
Buttonhole row Rib 9, [work 2 tog, yo, rib 13] 5 times, work 2 tog, yo, rib 9.

Work a further 5 rows.
Change to size 5 (3.75mm) needles.
Beg with a K row, work 60 rows in St st.
Bind off.

FINISHING

Back: Lap upper back rib over lower back rib and baste in place.
With RS together, sew back to front. Turn to RS, sew on buttons.
Insert cushion pad.

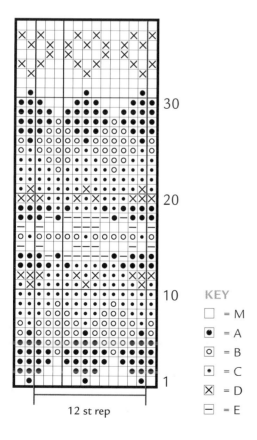

12 st rep

KEY

☐ = M
⦿ = A
◉ = B
⊡ = C
☒ = D
⊟ = E

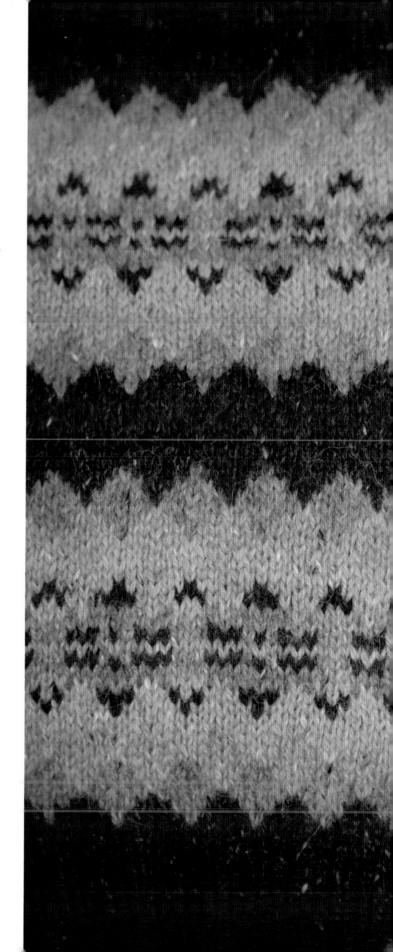

KYRIE

I never really believed that legwarmers were functional, I always thought they were a fashion accessory. In fact, they serve both purposes. Extra warmth around your calves when walking or gardening keeps your muscles loose and helps them to function well. So, when you knit these legwarmers, for yourself or a hiking or gardening friend, you will be doing them a good favor! Knitting them in a bright but soft green seems to be just right for a country look.

FINISHED SIZE

To fit an average woman's (man's) leg
Approx. length 20½in/52cm

YARN

4 x 1¾oz/197yd balls of Rowan *Felted Tweed* in
Avocado 161

NEEDLES

Pair of size 3 (3.25mm) knitting needles
Pair of size 5 (3.75mm) knitting needles
Cable needle

GAUGE

23 sts and 32 rows to 4in/10cm square measured
over St st using size 5 (3.75mm) needles *or size to
obtain correct gauge.*
33 sts and 32 rows to 4in/10cm square measured
over cable patt using size 5 (3.75mm) needles *or size
to obtain correct gauge.*

ABBREVIATIONS

See page 133.

SPECIAL ABBREVIATIONS

C4B = cable 4 back, slip next 2 sts on a cable needle
and leave at back of work, K2, then K2 from cable
needle; **C4F** = cable 4 front, slip next 2 sts on a cable
needle and leave at front of work, K2, then K2 from
cable needle; **C4R** = cross 4 right, slip next 2 sts on
a cable needle and leave at back of work, K2, then
P2 from cable needle; **C4L** = cross 4 left, slip next 2
sts on a cable needle and leave at front of work, P2,
then K2 from cable needle; **C3R** = cross 3 right, slip
next st on a cable needle and leave at back of work,
K2, then P1 from cable needle; **C3L** = cross 3 left,
slip next 2 sts on a cable needle and leave at front of
work, P1, then K2 from cable needle.

Patt Panel A (worked over 20 sts)

Row 1 K2, P4, [C4B] twice, P4, K2.
Row 2 P2, K4, P8, K4, P2.
Row 3 K2, P2, C4R, C4B, C4L, P2, K2.
Row 4 [P2, K2] twice, P4, [K2, P2] twice.
Row 5 [K2, P2] twice, K4, [P2, K2] twice.
Row 6 As row 4.
Row 7 [K2, P2] twice, C4B, [P2, K2] twice.
Rows 8 to 19 Rep rows 4 to 7 three times.
Row 20 As row 4.
Row 21 As row 5.
Row 22 As row 4.
Row 23 K2, P2, C4L, C4B, C4R, P2, K2.
Row 24 P2, K4, P8, K4, P2.
Rows 25 to 112 Rep rows 1 to 24 three times more
then rows 1 to 16 again.

These 112 rows form the patt panel.

Patt Panel B (worked over 32 sts)

Row 1 P12, [C4F] twice, P12.
Row 2 K12, P8, K12.
Row 3 P11, C3R, K4, C3L, P11.
Row 4 K11, P2, K1, P4, K1, P2, K11.
Row 5 P10, C3R, P1, C4B, P1, C3L, P10.
Row 6 K10, P2, K2, P4, K2, P2, K10.
Row 7 P9, C3R, P1, C3R, C3L, P1, C3L, P9.
Row 8 K9, [P2, K2] 3 times, P2, K9.
Row 9 P8, C3R, P1, C3R, P2, C3L, P1, C3L, P8.
Row 10 K8, P2, K2, P2, K4, P2, K2, P2, K8.
Row 11 P7, C3R, P1, C3R, P4, C3L, P1, C3L, P7.
Row 12 K7, P2, K2, P2, K6, P2, K2, P2, K7.
Row 13 P6, C3R, P1, C3R, P6, C3L, P1, C3L, P6.
Row 14 K6, P2, K2, P2, K8, P2, K2, P2, K6.
Row 15 P5, C3R, P1, C3R, P8, C3L, P1, C3L, P5.
Row 16 K5, P2, K2, P2, K10, P2, K2, P2, K5.
Row 17 P4, C3R, P1, C3R, P10, C3L, P1, C3L, P4.
Row 18 K4, P2, K2, P2, K12, P2, K2, P2, K4.
Row 19 P3, C3R, P1, C3R, P12, C3L, P1, C3L, P3.
Row 20 K3, P2, K2, P2, K14, P2, K2, P2, K3.
Row 21 P2, C3R, P1, C3R, P14, C3L, P1, C3L, P2.
Row 22 K2, P2, K2, P2, K16, P2, K2, P2, K2.

Row 23 P2, C3L, C3R, P16, C3L, C3R, P2.

Row 24 K3, P4, K18, P4, K3.

Row 25 P3, C4B, P18, C4F, P3.

Row 26 As row 24.

Row 27 P2, C3R, C3L, P16, C3R, C3L, P2.

Row 28 As row 22.

Row 29 P2, C3L, P1, C3L, P14, C3R, P1, C3R, P2.

Row 30 As row 20

Row 31 P3, C3L, P1, C3L, P12, C3R, P1, C3R, P3.

Row 32 As row 18.

Row 33 P4, C3L, P1, C3L, P10, C3R, P1, C3R, P4.

Row 34 As row 16.

Row 35 P5, C3L, P1, C3L, P8, C3R, P1, C3R, P5.

Row 36 As row 14.

Row 37 P6, C3L, P1, C3L, P6, C3R, P1, C3R, P6.

Row 38 As row 12.

Row 39 P7, C3L, P1, C3L, P4, C3R, P1, C3R, P7.

Row 40 As row 10.

Row 41 P8, C3L, P1, C3L, P2, C3R, P1, C3R, P8.

Row 42 As row 8.

Row 43 P9, C3L, P1, C3L, C3R, P1, C3R, P9.

Row 44 As row 6.

Row 45 P10, C3L, P1, C4B, P1, C3R, P10.

Row 46 As row 4.

Row 47 P11, C3L, K4, C3R, P11.

Row 48 K12, P8, K12.

Rows 49 to 112 Rep rows 1 to 48 once more then rows 1 to 16 again.

These 112 rows form the patt panel.

LEGWARMERS (make 2)

Using size 3 (3.25mm) needles cast on 82 (90) sts.

Row 1 (RS) K2, [P2, K2] to end.

Row 2 P2, [K2, P2] to end.

These 2 rows form rib.

Work a further 28 rows.

Change to size 5 (3.75mm) needles and patt.

Row 1 P5 (9), work 1st row of Patt Panel A, Patt Panel B, Patt Panel A, P5 (9).

Row 2 K5 (9), work 2nd row of Patt Panel A, Patt Panel B, Patt Panel A, K5 (9).

These 2 rows set the position for the patt panels.

Work a further 10 rows.

Inc row P6, M1pw, patt to last 6 sts, M1pw, P6.

Work a further 11 rows.

Rep the last 12 rows 6 times more and the inc row again. *98 (106) sts.*

Work even until 112 rows have been worked in patt.

Change to size 3 (3.25mm) needles.

Row 1 (RS) K2, [P2, K2] to end.

Row 2 P2, [K2, P2] to end.

These 2 rows form rib.

Work a further 28 rows.

Bind off in rib.

FINISHING

Join back seam (see page 133).

LOTTA

This is a subtle but very pretty
dotted pattern, using four colors,
in which the bands at the ends of
the scarf reverse the colorways.
As the scarf is double thickness,
knitted in Rowan Felted Tweed,
it is really warm. The scarf ends
are finished in garter stitch with
long fringes worked by knitting
long strings of three stitches, with
three stitches in between.

FINISHED SIZE
8¼ x 56¼in/21 x 143cm (excluding fringe)

YARN
4 x 1¾oz/197yd balls of Rowan *Felted Tweed* in Gilt 160 (A)

1 x 1¾oz/197yd ball of Rowan *Felted Tweed* in Watery 152 (B)

1 x 1¾oz/197yd ball of Rowan *Felted Tweed* in Melody 142 (C)

1 x 1¾oz/197yd ball of Rowan *Felted Tweed* in Avocado 161 (D)

NEEDLES
Pair of size 5 (3.75mm) knitting needles
Two short double-pointed size 3 (3.25mm) knitting needles

GAUGE
24 sts and 30 rows to 4in/10cm square measured over patterned St st using size 5 (3.75mm) needles *or size to obtain correct gauge.*

ABBREVIATIONS
See page 133.

NOTE
When working from Chart, odd numbered rows are K rows and read from right to left. Even numbered rows are P rows and read from left to right. When working from Chart use the intarsia method. Use a small separate ball of yarn for each area of color, twisting the yarns on wrong side when changing color to avoid a hole.

SCARF
Using size 5 (3.75mm) needles and B cast on 100 sts.

Row 1 Using B, K to end.

Row 2 Using B, P to end.

Row 3 K5B, [work across row 1 of Chart A, K6B] 7 times, work across row 1 of Chart A, K5B.

Row 4 P5B, [work across row 2 of Chart A, P6B] 7 times, work across row 2 of Chart A, P5B.

These 2 rows set the positions of Chart A.

Rows 5 to 8 Work as set to end of Chart.

Rows 9 to 16 Rep rows 1 and 2 four times.

Row 17 K11B, [work across row 1 of Chart A, K6B] 6 times, work across row 1 of Chart A, K11B.

Row 18 P11B, [work across row 2 of Chart A, P6B] 6 times, work across row 2 of Chart A, P11B.

These 2 rows set the positions of Chart A.

Rows 19 to 22 Work as set to end of Chart.

Rows 23 to 30 Rep rows 1 and 2 four times.

Rows 31 to 38 As rows 3 to 10.

Row 39 Using A, K to end.

Row 40 Using A, P to end.

Rows 41 to 44 Rep rows 39 and 40 twice.

Row 45 K11A, [work across row 1 of Chart B, K6A] 6 times, work across row 1 of Chart B, K11A.

Row 46 P11A, [work across row 2 of Chart B, P6A] 6 times, work across row 2 of Chart B, P11A.

These 2 rows set the positions of the Chart B.

Rows 47 to 50 Work as set to end of Chart.

Rows 51 to 58 Rep rows 39 and 40 four times.

Row 59 K5A, [work across row 1 of Chart B, K6A] 7 times, work across row 1 of Chart B, K5A.

Row 60 P5A, [work across row 2 of Chart B, P6A] 7 times, work across row 2 of Chart B, P5A.

These 2 rows set the positions of the Chart B.

Rows 61 to 64 Work as set to end of Chart.

Rows 65 to 72 Rep rows 39 and 40 four times.

Rows 73 to 392 Rep rows 45 to 72 eleven times more then rows 45 to 56 again.

Chart A   Chart B   KEY

☐ = A
☒ = B
◉ = C
⬤ = D

Rows 393 to 430 As rows 1 to 38.
Bind off.

FINISHING
Join row ends together.
With seam running down center of back, using size 3 (3.25mm) double-pointed needles and A, working through both thicknesses pick up and K48 sts along one short end.
K 6 rows.
Next row * K3, [slide these 3 sts to other end of needle, K3] 60 times, K3tog and fasten off; rep from * to end of row.
Work other end to match.

BODIE

This smart shopper-style big bag has a great all-over checkerboard pattern in Rowan Felted Tweed in dark green and bronze. The Fair Isle stranded color technique used here looks almost as though it has been woven. A cardboard liner in the base gives the bag extra strength.

FINISHED SIZE

Approx. 16½ x 13in/42 x 33cm

YARN

3 x 1¾oz/197yd balls of Rowan *Felted Tweed* in Pine 158 (A)

2 x 1¾oz/197yd balls of Rowan *Felted Tweed* in Gilt 160 (B)

NEEDLES

Pair of size 5 (3.75mm) knitting needles

EXTRAS

49¼in/125cm of 1in/2.5cm wide petersham ribbon
Lining fabric, 19¾ x 47¼in/50 x 120cm
Microfiber batting (¹/₈in/3mm thick), 19¾ x 47¼in/50 x 120cm
Cardboard for base of bag

GAUGE

25 sts and 27 rows to 4in/10cm square over patt using size 5 (3.75mm) needles *or size to obtain correct gauge.*

ABBREVIATIONS

See page 133.

BACK AND FRONT (both alike)

Using size 5 (3.75mm) needles and A cast on 107 sts.

Row 1 K6A, [5B, 5A] to last 11 sts, 5B, 6A.
Row 2 P2A, [1B, 1A] to last 3 sts, 1B, 2A.
Row 3 K3A, [1B, 2A, 2B, 1A, 2B, 2A] to last 4 sts, 1B, 3A.
Row 4 As row 2.
Row 5 As row 1.
Row 6 P6B, [5A, 5B] to last 11 sts, 5A, 6B.
Row 7 K2B, [1A, 1B] to last 3 sts, 1A, 2B.
Row 8 P3B, [1A, 2B, 2A, 1B, 2A, 2B] to last 4 sts, 1A, 3B.
Row 9 As row 7.

Row 10 As row 6.
These 10 rows form the 10 row patt rep.
Cont in patt until 85 rows have been worked.
Cont in A only.
Dec row P2, [P3, P2tog] 20 times, P5. *87 sts.*
P 3 rows.
Bind off.

SIDES (make 2)

Using size 5 (3.75mm) needles and B cast on 27 sts.

Row 1 K6B, 5A, 5B, 5A, 6B.
Row 2 P2B, [1A, 1B] to last 3 sts, 1A, 2B.
Row 3 K3B, [1A, 2B, 2A, 1B, 2A, 2B] to last 4 sts, 1A, 3B.
Row 4 As row 2.
Row 5 As row 1.
Row 6 P6A, 5B, 5A, 5B, 6A.
Row 7 K2A, [1B, 1A] to last 3 sts, 1B, 2A.
Row 8 P3A, [1B, 2A, 2B, 1A, 2B, 2A] to last 4 sts, 1B, 3A.
Row 9 As row 7.
Row 10 As row 6.
These 10 rows form the patt rep.
Cont in patt until 85 rows have been worked.
Cont in A only.
Dec row P3, [P2, P2tog] 5 times, P4. *22 sts.*
P 3 rows.
Bind off.

BASE

Using size 5 (3.75mm) needles and A cast on 24 sts.
Beg with a K row, cont in St st until work—unstretched—fits from along cast-on edges of front and back, ending with a P row.
Bind off.

HANDLE (make 2)

Using size 5 (3.75mm) needles and A cast on 21 sts.

Next row K5, sl 1pw, K9, sl 1pw, K5.
Next row P to end.
Rep the last 2 rows until strip measures
23½in/60cm, ending with a P row.
Bind off.

FINISHING

Using knitted pieces as templates and adding seam
allowance, cut out front, back, sides, and base from
the lining and batting. Baste batting to lining and
use as one piece.
Sew ends of base to cast-on edges of sides. Sew row
ends of sides to row ends of back and front. Sew
base to cast-on edges of back and front.

Make up lining in same way.
Place petersham ribbon along center of WS of
handle and slip stitch in place along knitted slipped
sts. Bring row ends of handle together encasing
petersham ribbon and sew row ends together to
form seam.
Sew handles to inside of back and front 4¾in/12cm
apart.
Place lining inside bag, fold seam allowance to WS
and slip stitch lining in place.
For extra stiffness in bottom of bag cut a piece of
cardboard to fit base. From lining make a "bag" to
cover cardboard. Place in bottom of bag.

Colorwork Knitting

There are two main methods of working with color in knitted fabrics: the intarsia and the Fair Isle techniques. The first method produces a single thickness of fabric and is usually used where a new color is required for a block of stitches and rows in a particular area of a piece of knitting. Where a small repeating color pattern of up to 3 or 4 stitches is created across the row, the Fair Isle technique is generally used. Almost all the patterns in this book use the Fair Isle technique.

Intarsia

In the intarsia technique, you have to join in a new yarn color for each new block of color stitches. To prevent the yarns getting twisted on the ball, the simplest method is to make individual little balls of yarn, or bobbins, from pre-cut short lengths of yarn, one for each motif or block of color used in a row. You then work across the stitches, joining in the colors as required, by twisting them around each other where they meet on the wrong side of the work, to avoid gaps.

After you have completed the piece of knitting, you need to neaten up the loose ends. They can either be darned along the color joins or knitted in to the fabric as each color is worked by picking up the loops of the yarns carried across the back of the work as you knit. The Reindeer motif, shown right, is a mixture of intarsia and Fair Isle techniques. Intarsia is used for the body of the reindeer (to avoid carrying the yarns across too many stitches) and the Fair Isle technique for the repeating areas of pattern.

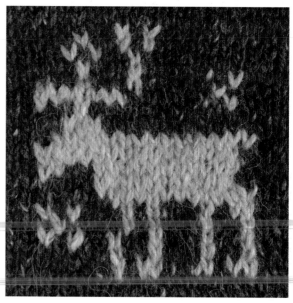

The Reindeer motif is worked using intarsia for the body and Fair Isle for the rest of the motif.

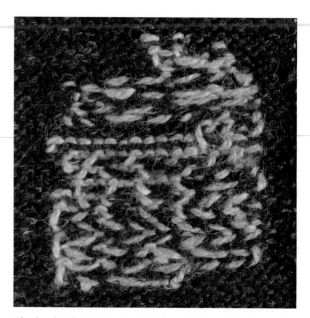

The back of the Reindeer: the cut yarns of the Intarsia parts are darned in after the motif has been worked.

The front of the Astrid design using the Fair Isle technique.

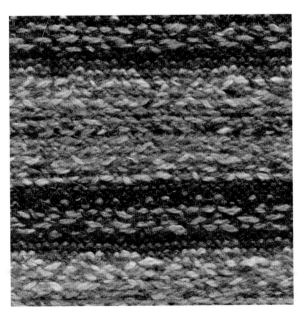

The back of the Astrid design showing the evenly stranded yarns.

Fair Isle

When you are working a pattern with two or more repeating colors in the same row, you need to strand the yarn not in use behind the stitches being worked. This needs to be done with care, loosely enough to ensure that the strands not in use do not tighten and pucker the front of the knitting. To do this you need to treat the yarns not in use, known as "floating yarns," as if they were one yarn and spread the stitches as you work to their correct width to keep them elastic.

If your pattern demands that the stranded or floating yarns are carried across more than three stitches, it is wise to weave the new yarn color under and over the color yarn you are working with each time you change colors (over the first time, under the second time, and so on). The alternating "under and over" movement helps to prevent the floating yarns from tangling by keeping them caught at the back of the work.

It is important when knitting with more than one color to keep your gauge correct, as it easy to pull the loops of yarn too tight, puckering the work. If you tend to knit colorwork too tightly, increase your needle size for the colorwork section.

If you make a minor mistake using the Fair Isle techique—say, just a single stitch—you can recreate it in the correct color using the Swiss darning technique, in which you duplicate the stitch using a darning needle and the chosen color.

Pattern Information

SIZING

The instructions are given for the smallest size, and larger sizes follow in parentheses. If there is only one set of figures, it refers to all sizes. If - (hyphen) or 0 (zero) is given in an instruction for the size you are knitting, then that particular instruction does not apply to your size.

Included with each garment pattern in this book is a size diagram of the finished garment pieces and their dimensions. The size diagram shows the finished width of the garment at the underarm point, and it is this measurement that you should choose first; a useful tip is to measure one of your own garments that is a comfortable fit. Having chosen a size based on width, look at the corresponding length for that size; if you are not happy with the total recommended length, adjust your own garment before beginning your armhole shaping—any adjustment after this point will mean that your sleeve will not fit into your garment easily. Don't forget to take your adjustment into account if there is any side-seam shaping.

GAUGE

Obtaining the correct gauge can make the difference between a successful garment and a disastrous one. It controls both the shape and size of an article, so any variation, however slight, can distort the finished garment.

You must match the gauge given at the start of each pattern. To check your gauge, knit a square in the pattern stitch and/or stockinette stitch of perhaps 5–10 more stitches and 5–10 more rows than those given in the gauge note. Press the finished square under a damp cloth and mark out the central 4in/10cm square with pins. If you have too many stitches to 4in/10cm, try again using thicker needles. If you have too few stitches to 4in/10cm, try again using finer needles. Once you have achieved the correct gauge, your garment will be knitted to the measurements shown in the size diagram with the pattern.

CHART NOTES

Many patterns in this book are worked from charts. Each square of the chart represents a stitch and each line of squares represents a row of knitting. Each color used is given a different letter in a key alongside the chart and these letters are shown too in the list of yarns used in each pattern. When working from charts, read odd-numbered rows (K) from right to left and even numbered rows (P) from left to right, unless otherwise stated.

CABLE PATTERNS

Cable stitch patterns allow you to twist the stitches in various ways, to create decorative effects such as an interesting ropelike structure to the knitting. The cables can be thin and fine (just a couple of stitches wide) or really big and chunky (up to 8 stitches or more).

To work cables, you need to hold the appropriate number of stitches that form the cable twist (abbreviated in pattern as C) on a separate small cable needle, while you knit behind or in front of them. You then knit the stitches off the cable needle before continuing to knit the remaining stitches in the row. Depending on whether the cable needle is at the front or the back of the work, the cables will twist to the left or right but the principle remains the same. A four-stitch cable will be abbreviated as C4F or C4B, depending on whether the cable needle is held to the front or back of the work.

FINISHING METHODS

Pressing

Block out each piece of knitting by pinning it on a board to the correct measurements in the pattern. Then lightly press it according to the ball band instructions, omitting any ribbed areas.

Take special care to press the edges, as this makes sewing up easier and neater. If you cannot press the fabric, then cover the knitted fabric with a damp cloth and let stand for a couple of hours.

Darn in all ends neatly along the selvedge edge or a color join, as appropriate.

Stitching seams

When you stitch the pieces together, remember to match any areas of color and texture carefully where they meet. Use a special seam stitch, called mattress stitch, as it creates the neatest flattest seam. After all the seams are complete, press the seams and hems.

Lastly, sew on the buttons to correspond with the positions of the buttonholes.

Making linings for bags

If you are knitting the bags in this book, it pays to line them carefully, using appropriate fabric. A good quality strong cotton is ideal for knitted bags as it provides some support for the fabric. Where the bag has a gusset at the base, you can add some extra strength to the base in the form of a cardboard liner, cut to the same size as the gusset. As you cannot wash the cardboard, you need to construct the liner for it so you can remove the cardboard easily.

It also pays to strengthen the straps of any bigger bags by wrapping the knitted pieces around a length of petersham ribbon, to make them less stretchy.

ABBREVIATIONS

The knitting pattern abbreviations used in this book are as below.

alt	alternate
approx.	approximate
beg	begin(s)(ning)
cm	centimeters
cont	continu(e)(ing)
dec	decreas(e)(ing)
foll	follow(s)(ing)
garter st	garter stitch (K every row)
in	inch(es)
inc	increas(e)(ing)
K	knit
K2tog	knit next 2 sts together
m	meter(s)
M1	make one stitch by picking up horizontal loop before next stitch and knitting into back of it
M1P	make one stitch by picking up horizontal loop before next stitch and purling into back of it
mm	millimeters
pw	purlwise
P	purl
patt	pattern
psso	pass slipped stitch over
p2sso	pass two slipped stitches over
P2tog	purl next 2 sts together
rem	remain(s)(ing)
rep	repeat
rev St st	reverse stockinette stitch
RS	right side
skp	sl 1, K1, psso
sl 1	slip one stitch
st(s)	stitch(es)
St st	stockinette stitch (1 row K, 1 row P)
tbl	through back of loop(s)
tog	together
WS	wrong side
yd	yard(s)
yo	yarn over right needle to make a new stitch

Yarn Information

The yarns used in this book are all Rowan yarns. If you decide to substitute a yarn or yarns, take great care to check the gauge to make sure it matches the pattern. Knit a swatch to test the gauge and, if necessary, reduce or increase your needle size to achieve the same gauge as the pattern.

Rowan *Classic Cashsoft 4-ply*

A superfine-weight wool-and-cashmere mix yarn; 57 percent fine merino wool, 33 percent microfiber, 10 percent cashmere; 1¾oz/50g (approximately 197yd/180m) per ball. Recommended gauge: 28sts and 36 rows to 4in/10cm measured over St st using size 3 (3¼mm) knitting needles.

Rowan *Cocoon*

A medium weight merino-mohair mix; 80 percent merino, 20 percent kid mohair; 100g/2oz (126yd/115m) per ball; recommended gauge: 14sts and 16 rows to 4in/10cm measured over St st using size 10½ (7mm) knitting needles.

Rowan *Felted Tweed*

A lightweight wool-alpaca-viscose mix; 50 percent merino wool, 25 percent alpaca wool, 25 percent viscose; 1¾oz/50g (approximately 191yd/175m) per ball. Recommended gauge: 22–24 sts and 30–32 rows to 4in/10cm measured over St st using size 5–6 (3¼–4mm) knitting needles.

Rowan *Felted Tweed Chunky*

A lightweight wool-alpaca-viscose mix; 50 percent merino wool, 25 percent alpaca wool, 25 percent viscose; 1¾oz/50g (approximately 55yd/50m) per ball. Recommended gauge: 11 sts and 14 rows to 4in/10cm measured over St st using size 11 (8mm) knitting needles.

Rowan *Felted Tweed Aran*

An Aran weight merino wool-alpaca-viscose mix yarn; 50 percent merino wool, 25 percent alpaca, 15 percent viscose; 1¾oz/50g (95yd/87m) per ball. Recommended gauge: 16sts and 23 rows to 4in/10cm measured over St st using size 8 (5mm) knitting needles.

Rowan *Kidsilk Haze*

A fine-weight mohair mix yarn; 70 percent super kid mohair, 30 percent silk; ⅞oz/25g (approximately 229yd/210m) per ball. Recommended gauge: 18–25 sts and 23–34 rows to 4in/10cm measured over St st using size 3–8 (3¼–5mm) knitting needles.

Rowan *Wool Cotton*

A lightweight wool/cotton blend yarn; 50 percent merino wool, 50 percent cotton; 1¾oz/50g (approximately 123yd/113m) per ball; recommended gauge: 22–24sts and 30–32 rows to 4in/10cm measured over St st using size 5–6 (3¼–4mm) knitting needles.

Buying Yarns

Rowan yarns (and buttons) have been used for all the knitting patterns in this book. See opposite for descriptions of the yarns used. To find out where to buy Rowan yarns near you, contact one of the Rowan yarn distributors given below. The main Rowan office is in the United Kingdom (see below for their website).

ROWAN YARN DISTRIBUTORS

U.S.A.
Westminster Fibers Inc,
165 Ledge Street, Nashua,
New Hampshire 03060
Tel: 1-800-445-9276
www.westminsterfibers.com

U.K.
Rowan, Green Lane Mill, Holmfirth,
West Yorkshire, HD9 2DX
Tel: +44 (0) 1484 681881
Fax: +44 (0) 1484 687920
Email: mail@knitrowan.com
www.knitrowan.com

AUSTRALIA
Australian Country Spinners,
Pty Ltd,
Level 7, 409 St. Kilda Road,
Melbourne Vic 3004
Tel: 03 9380 3830
Fax: 03 9820 0989
Email: sales@auspinners.com.au

AUSTRIA
Coats Harlander GmbH,
Autokaderstrasse 31,
A-1210 Wien.
Tel: (01) 27716 - 0
Fax: (01) 27716 - 228

BELGIUM
Coats Benelux, Ring Oost 14A,
Ninove, 9400, Belgium
Tel: 0346 35 37 00
Email: sales.coatsninove@coats.com

CANADA
Westminster Fibers Inc,
165 Ledge Street, Nashua,
New Hampshire 03060
Tel: 1-800-445-9276
www.westminsterfibers.com

CHINA
Coats Shanghai Ltd, No 9 Building,
Baosheng Road,
Songjiang Industrial Zone, Shanghai.
Tel: (86-21) 5774 3733
Fax: (86-21) 5774 3768

DENMARK
Coats Danmark A/S,
Nannasgade 28,
2200 Kobenhavn N
Tel: (45) 35 86 90 50
Fax: (45) 35 82 15 10
Email: info@hpgruppen.dk
www.hpgruppen.dk

FINLAND
Coats Opti Oy, Ketjutie 3,
04220 Kerava
Tel: (358) 9 274 871
Fax: (358) 9 2748 7330
Email: coatsopti.sales@coats.com

FRANCE
Coats France / Steiner Frères,
SAS 100, avenue du Général de Gaulle,
18 500 Mehun-Sur-Yèvre
Tel: (33) 02 48 23 12 30
Fax: (33) 02 48 23 12 40

GERMANY
Coats GmbH, Kaiserstrasse 1,
D-79341 Kenzingen
Tel: (49) 7644 8020
Fax: (49) 7644 802399
www.coatsgmbh.de

HOLLAND
Coats Benelux, Ring Oost 14A,
Ninove, 9400, Belgium
Tel: 0346 35 37 00
Email: sales.coatsninove@coats.com

HONG KONG
Coats China Holdings Ltd,
19/F Millennium City 2,
378 Kwun Tong Road,
Kwun Tong, Kowloon
Tel: (852) 2798 6886
Fax: (852) 2305 0311

ICELAND
Storkurinn, Laugavegi 59,
101 Reykjavik
Tel: (354) 551 8258
Email: storkurinn@simnet.is

ITALY
Coats Cucirini s.r.l., Via Sarca 223,
20126 Milano
Tel: 800 992377
Fax: 0266111701
Email: servizio.clienti@coats.com

KOREA
Coats Korea Co Ltd, 5F Kuckdong
B/D, 935-40 Bangbae-Dong,
Seocho-Gu, Seoul
Tel: (82) 2 521 6262.
Fax: (82) 2 521 5181

Acknowledgments

AUTHOR'S ACKNOWLEDGMENTS

Martin Storey would like to specially thank: Lucy and Rob Wakefield for the use of their wonderful home; Penny Hill and her team of knitters for the beautifully knitted designs featured in this book; Jackie Wright for her invaluable help on knitting the swatches; Kate Buller and Marie Wallin at Rowan for their continuous support.

PUBLISHERS' ACKNOWLEDGMENTS

The publishers would like to thank Anne Wilson for graphic design; John Heseltine for photography; Katie Hardwicke for editing; Penny Hill, Marilyn Wilson for pattern writing and checking respectively; Lisa Richardson for diagrams; Ed Berry for charts; and Lucy, Morwenna, Nathalie, and Ed for modeling.